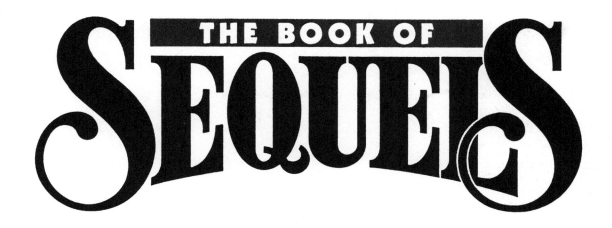

THE BOOK OF SEQUELS

by Henry Beard, Christopher Cerf, Sarah Durkee, and Sean Kelly

with Chris Kelly, John Korkes, and Norman Stiles

Art Directed and Designed by David Kaestle, Inc.

A Joint Project of
THE AMERICAN SEQUEL SOCIETY
and RANDOM HOUSE

New York

**Produced by Christopher Cerf Associates, Inc.
in association with David Kaestle Inc.**

Editors
Christopher Cerf and Henry Beard

Executive Art Director
David Kaestle

Art Director
David Vogler

Book Design
David Kaestle and Diane Bertolo

Production Supervisor
Donna Cisan

Production Artists
Linda Neaman and David Wilson

Special Thanks to:
Jennifer Ash; Jonathan Becker; Dona Chernoff; Gwyneth Cravens;
Victor Di Napoli; Janis Donnaud; Bruce Harris;
Jim Henson Productions, Inc.; Kent Holland; Mitchell Ivers;
Paul Jacobs; Linda Kaye; Bernie Klein; Lincoln Scenic Studio, Inc.;
Rick Meyerowitz; Lesley Oelsner; Beth Pearson; Jill Rabon;
Nancy Sans; Carol Schneider; Trish Todd;
and especially Joni Evans, David Rosenthal and Ed Victor

All rights reserved under International and Pan-American
Copyright Conventions. Published in the United States by
Random House, Inc., New York and simultaneously in Canada by
Random House of Canada Limited, Toronto.

Library of Congress Cataloging-in-Publication Data
The Book of sequels/by Henry Beard, Christopher Cerf,
Sarah Durkee, and Sean Kelly.
p. ca.
ISBN 0-394-58841-7
1. Sequels (Literature)—Humor. 2. Motion picture sequels—Humor.
I. Beard, Henry. II. Cerf, Christopher. III. Durkee, Sarah.
IV. Kelly, Sean. V. Title.
PN6231, S497866 1990
817′.5407—dc20 90-53150

Manufactured in the United States of America
98765432 24689753 24356789
First Edition

A project of the Dynamite Museum.

Contents

Introduction	5
Back with the Wind	6
The Scarlett Fanny	8
Slaves of Atlanta	10
Southern Bellefleur	13
The Color Scarlett	14
A Gallery of Sequel Book Covers	17
First Communion	17
Diuretics	17
The Stephen King Book-of-the-Week Club	18
Vegetable Farm	19
Pride and Extreme Prejudice	19
Solitude: The Next One Hundred Years	20
The Princess	27
Finn Fin	30
The Way Things Break	31
Sir Gawain and the Green Knight at the Opera	32
Go Kindly and Gently Into That Good Night	35
The One Bullet Manager: The Management Secrets of the Khmer Rouge	36
The Return of the Gift of the Magi	40
Judaism and the Art of Motorcycle Maintenance	42
Casey II: It Ain't Over Till It's Over	44
Two Cities II: The Tale Continues	45
Number One, With a Bullet: The Untold Story of Joyce Kilmer's Unfinished Sequel to His Immortal Masterpiece, "Trees"	48
That's Re-Entertainment	50
Movie Sequels/The Rocky Awards	52
Force 10 from Casablanca	53
2000: A Space Iliad	54
I Was a Teenage Beowulf	55
The Big Fat Balding Prince	56
The Man Who Would Be Queen	61
The Library of Yiddish Sequels (*advertisement*)	66
Brideshead Revisited Revisited	68

Contents: The Final Page

Answers to the Letters of George Bernard Shaw   72

Everything You Wanted to Know About Sacks*
    *But Were So Aphasic You Forgot to Ask   74

Thus Joked Zarathustra (Also spasst Zarathustra)   75

Romeo and Juliet, Part 1 (cont.)   76

Aristotle's Aerobics   79

The Lighter Side of Sylvia Plath   83

The Ed Norton Anthology of Underground Poetry Sequels   84
    The Emperor of Frozen Yogurt   84
    What I Scribe—Here in Amherst   85
    The Road Taken   85

A Brief History of Art and Architecture Sequels
    The Triumph of the Familiar   86

Moby-Dick II: Raise the Pequod!   92

The Egyptian Flip Book of the Dead   94

The Idiot Sequels (advertisement)   123

Spin-Offs/Culture: The Next Generation   124
    The Strange Case of Dr. Jekyll and Mr. Heckle   125
    T.S. Eliot's™ Wasteland Theme Park   126

The Satanic Reverses   128

Godot Action Comics   130

The Chain Letter of Paul the Apostle to the Corinthians   135

The Word-a-Day in the Life of Ivan Denisovich Calendar   136

Adult Sequels   137

How They Faxed the Good News from Ghent to Aix   138

Existendo™ Video Games   139

Literary Strips and Philosophical Funnies   140
    Bloomsbury   140
    Hobbes and Calvin   140

Toronto   141

Make Your Own Sequel™:
    New Beginnings, Next Chapters and Continuing Nightmares   142

Index of Credits   144

Introduction

Congratulations!

You have shown the wisdom and good taste to open—and begin reading the introduction to—a book with historic literary implications.

What impels us to make such an immodest assertion? Luckily, there is no need for us to answer that question, because the material we have assembled in these pages speaks far more eloquently than we ever could. Here, read me, it says, and you will discover that the sequel and its intellectual cousins the prequel, the spin-off, the tie-in, the themed attraction, and the licensed product are not, as has been alleged, mere "cultural stepchildren," but legitimate art forms in their own right, each as deserving of critical respect as any of the more traditionally accepted modes of creative expression.

Indeed, it is difficult to understand why sons-of, Part IIs, updates, returns-of, revenges-of, and their ilk ever fell into disrepute in the first place, for some of the world's acknowledged masterpieces have been sequels. What was Homer's beloved epic, *The Odyssey,* for example, if not the "continuing adventures of" Ulysses, the hero the poet introduced so successfully in *The Iliad*? Sophocles followed up his groundbreaking tragedy *Oedipus Rex* with the equally acclaimed *Oedipus at Colonus* and *Antigone*—plays that he might well have called *Oedipus II* and *Oedipus III,* had Roman numerals been invented. And the great Bard himself, William Shakespeare, wrote innumerable sequels, including *Henry IV, Part 2; Henry V; Henry VI, Part 1; Henry VI, Part 2; Henry VI, Part 3;* and *Romeo and Juliet, Part 2* (the startling discovery of which is discussed in detail in this book). We owe these "great sequelizers" an eternal debt—a debt that we intend to begin repaying now, by dedicating our book to them, and by doing our level best to follow (how appropriate!) in their hallowed footsteps.

So fervent is our zeal to return the sequel to its former glory that we have founded an organization—the American Sequel Society (or "A-Double-S," as we like to call it)—dedicated to ferreting out, or when necessary creating from scratch, as many quality sequels to beloved books and films as is humanly possible. Literally hundreds of these works are represented in the volume you hold in your hand.

Now, contrary to what some have suggested, the fact that Warner Books recently paid $4.9 million for the rights to a *Gone with the Wind* follow-up in no way influenced our decision to start the American Sequel Society. Yes, like all editor-entrepreneurs, we have a responsibility to our investors to turn a profit. But, in the great tradition of publishing pioneer Chris Whittle (whose ingenious concept of including advertising in books we have gratefully appropriated), we see no conflict between the twin goals of generating art and generating revenues.

But enough talk of high purpose and high finance. We conceived *The Book of Sequels* not merely to make a point (or a buck), but to entertain you, the reader, by bringing back—in new and, in many cases, improved form—the books and movies that, by your "votes" at the shopping mall and ticket booth, you've indicated you like the most. In a very real sense, *you* have created this book. And, if you ask us, you've done a truly bang-up job!

New York,
October 1990

BACK WITH THE WIND

Yes, we know Margaret Mitchell's immortal Civil War epic *Gone with the Wind* sold more than 176,000 copies within the first three weeks of its publication in 1936 and won the Pulitzer Prize the following year. True, it was purchased for the movies by MGM for an unprecedented sum and was made into a film that won ten Academy Awards and has been seen by well over a quarter of a billion people worldwide. Granted, it may well be the most beloved movie of all time. And yes, the book has sold over twenty-one million copies in thirty-one countries and has made Scarlett O'Hara and Rhett Butler arguably the most vivid pair of lovers in all of American literature. But...*is it a good bet for a sequel?*

Well, some people just seem to have a kind of sixth sense for what will "fly," and the gutsy folks at Warner Books, with just $4.9 million and a dream, thought there was evidence enough to take a gamble. And Alexandra Ripley, author of...well, many other things, set all else aside for the chance to write the sequel to *Gone with the Wind*. Why, you ask? Because they believed. And out of such courage and faith the true art of the sequel is born.

We salute you, Ms. Ripley. And it was with the same re-pioneering spirit of re-innovation in which artists like you dare put pen to recycled paper that the American Sequel Society decided to embark on its own very special project. What would happen, we wondered, if four of America's most respected contemporary women authors were invited to write *their* versions of a *Gone with the Wind* sequel? What literary treasures would result if, say, Erica Jong, Tama Janowitz, Joyce Carol Oates, and Alice Walker put *their* enormous talents to the task of updating the story of Scarlett and Rhett? Our letters to these authors were met with silence, our calls went unreturned, and our hopes dwindled. But just as we'd despaired of ever recruiting these women to our cause, we walked into the office one morning and found four manuscripts neatly stacked on the front desk. The authors' names appeared nowhere, but each piece was brilliantly written in a style we're sure readers will find instantly recognizable. They are, we think, masterpieces of the sequel art.
So to Erica, Tama, J.C. and Alice: Thank you.

Here, then, is a sampler of excerpts from these delightful sequels, each a loving tribute to an American classic that's finally back, back with the wind!

"Whoa, whoa, *whoa! Ouch!*"

I looked up scowling from where I lay across Big Jimbo's lap, mustering as imperious an air as possible for a woman whose raised hoopskirt gave the impression of a covered wagon. "Let's not be taking this too *far,* Master."

"What's dat you say, Miss Scarlett?" Jimbo cupped his ear mischievously, mocking me, and his perfect teeth flashed white in the night sky of his beautiful face.

And God help me, but I clung to his black thigh, thick as a cannon, and I batted the longest eyelashes in upcountry Georgia, and I begged in a whisper for that ol' tom-tom rhythm of his mammoth palm on my rosy backside again, again, *again*!

I've become, I confess, an absolutely ruthless businesswoman. This morning my accountant had gone over the figures for the lumber mills, and my profits were up 23 percent from 1868. Hurrah for the Recon-struction! Bless those Scalawags! Down the streets of Atlanta I pranced, smiling gaily at passersby in my secret knowledge that, as usual, I wasn't wearing any pantaloons. Bad, bad Scarlett on her way to see her dear, freed slave Big Jimbo for the punishment she deserved!

"You is a spoiled brat, Scarlett," he growled, and I squealed with delight as the smacks continued. "A naughty, naughty girl!"

"I know, I know!" I whimpered. "I'm rotten to the core!"

"Shallow . . ."

"Yes!"

"Manipulative . . ."

"Yes!"

"Childish . . ."

"Yes! Yes!"

"Sex-obsessed . . ."

"YES!"

And he flipped me over and gave me his warm mouth, and we crashed to the sawdust floor of his saddlery shop, and I came three times just looking at the pommels. And then, dear reader, he entered my beehive, my corncrib, my peach basket, my bunny hutch, my servants' quarters, my root cellar, my jelly jar, my pea patch, my squirrel's nest, my butter churn, my lumber mill, my honey cupboard, my duck blind, my sugar bowl, my julep pitcher, my milk pail, my *Lord*.

How did I get myself into these situations?

Don't let the name Scarlett O'Hara Hamilton Kennedy Butler Wilkes fool you. I've never had much need for men, and until Rhett Butler, little use for sex. But when that deepest part of a woman is touched, when a man lobs a torch into that gentle female pool of sexual naphtha, ah, reader, the lady will forever remember, and the lady can't walk normally for a week.

The day after Rhett left me *was,* indeed, another day. But not the day I'd imagined.

Ashley Wilkes came to me on his knees. On his knees!

A little brandy and I was down on mine, doing my bit for the Old South. Oh Ashley! Damp, restless dream of my girlhood!

"Marry me, Scarlett," he panted. "Dear, dense Melanie's dying wish was that I take care of you, and I've been so scathingly lonely these twenty-four hours past. Marry me, my darling! Marry me!"

And I could not speak, so full was my heart (and *nearly* full my mouth, for Ashley was proving a slight disappointment even then), but I nodded Yes! Yes!, so great was my gratitude at not having to start dating.

A hasty Mexican divorce followed, after which Rhett made an honest woman out of the crab-infested Belle Watling, who gave him the six kids he'd always wanted.

And Ashley and I were married at my beloved Tara.

Why, oh *why* can't a woman have every single solitary thing she dreams of, and constant fun, with absolutely no obliga-tions, no apologies, and no remorse?

It's a question that will forever baffle me.

So here you find Mrs. Wilkes today, thirty-one years old, furtively kissing Big Jimbo goodbye and shaking the sawdust out of her skirts.

When one dreads going home to one's prissy, boring husband, nothing will do but a visit to Mammy.

I love Mammy's office; so enveloping, so warm, so . . . *pudendal*. Like Mammy herself, who is now not only my Mammy, but also a therapist with a thriving practice.

"Lawdy, Scarlett. Ya'll sho' do git y'seff hopped up obah dem menfolks. Dat ol' unresolb'd relationship wib yo' daddy sho' be messin' you up good!"

"What do you think I should *do,* Mammy? Should I leave Ashley?"

"Whudda *y'all* think?"

"If only he were more like Rhett! Or Jimbo! Or the Tarleton twins! Or that yummy Yankee with the limp . . . or Cassandra with the riding crop over the

---

> *"Lawdy, Scarlett. Ya'll sho' do git y'seff hopped up obah dem menfolks. Dat ol' unresolb'd relationship wib yo' daddy sho' be messin' you up good!"*

---

saloon . . . or Judge Calvert . . . I'm meeting him in an hour . . . *he* slurps me up like I'm iced mint tea in *August* . . ."

"What ah be hearin' you sayin' is dat sex be a patho*logically* impo'tant bidness for y'all, Scarlett. Mebbe y'all should try thinkin' 'bout sumpin' *else* fo' a change."

"Fiddle-dee-dee!"

"Cut down on dat too, honey-chile. If de good Lawd wanted wimminfolks to be fiddlin' wib demseffs as much as *y'all* fiddle, He wouldn'a gibben 'em fingernails or menfolks!"

I sighed a sigh that shuddered all the way up from the pink soles of my feet, slid between my legs, curled across my soft belly, brushed my tingling breasts and lodged in my throat like a pubic hair. Perhaps it *was* a pubic hair. God, I was horny all of a sudden. Maybe I could just slip into Mammy's privy . . . hump the pictures of farm tools in the Fayetteville *Gazette* . . . that always relaxed me.

"Oh, Mammy, I just feel such *yearning* inside! And such terrible awful guilt! Why, if Ashley ever knew what kind of a wicked,

> ## "If Ashley ever knew what kind of a wicked, lusty, deceitful girl he married, he'd leave me in a minute!"

lusty, deceitful girl he married, he'd leave me in a minute!"

Mammy pondered this. I looked at a potted cactus on the windowsill and came.

"Mebbe dat's what y'all *want* him to do, Scarlett. Leave you! P'raps y'oughta write a *book,* honey! Hee, hee, hee! Git dat hot stuff down on papuh."

It was as if Mammy had lit a lamp in the dark chamber of my soul.

A book. I could write a book! About me, Scarlett! *My* thoughts, *my* feelings, *my* body functions! The things I love best!

And when Ashley reads it, he'll find out what a slut I am, and pack his bags . . .

My heart was racing. Naughty, naughty girl!

"Mammy, I'll do it! I'll *write* that book! I'll write *lots* of them, each with a heroine named . . . Charlotte O'Tara! So everybody will be *sure* it's me, though I'll deny it! Oh, Mammy, I'm so very, very excited! What on earth will people *think* of me?"

Mammy thought, and shook her head, and then began to utter those words I knew so well, though they dampened my enthusiasm not one whit!

"Frankly, Scarlett, dey won't gi . . ."

But I was flying to my writing desk! 𝍌

There was a joke that our friend Rhettie Lee told my little brother Gerald when he was five. It went, "Pete and Re-pete went out in a boat. Pete fell out. Who was left?" And when Gerald said "Re-pete," Rhettie started telling the joke all over again. Gerald kept falling for it again and again, saying "*Re*-pete!" He didn't know how to make the joke stop, it was like he was caught in some horrible existential loop, and he was only five.

But he did know where Aunt Pittypat

kept her little mother-of-pearl pistol, and while Rhettie Lee was laughing his head off and starting the joke over for the zillionth time, Gerald grabbed it from her underwear drawer, pointed it right between Rhettie Lee's eyes, and pulled the trigger.

My mother tells this story a lot, as if it somehow typifies Gerald. Or maybe it just typifies my mother, that she'd keep on telling the story, even though the fact that the pistol wasn't loaded might be the reason Gerald's been sort of depressed for the last twenty years. Rhett's in L.A. now, producing movies.

But what I think is, both the story *and* the telling of it typify the South, which is basically one big stupid green blender-drink of whims and obsessions. And Atlanta, where I live, tops it off like some dopey little paper umbrella.

My name is Scarlett, as in O'Hara, who actually happens to be an ancestor of ours. My mother's name is Scarlett, and then she had the incredible cruelty to name me Scarlett, so the line of Scarletts since that primo killer deb has remained unbroken since the Civil War. She says she couldn't help it. I guess I can understand the pressure. Plus, her side of the family is loaded. She still lives in Jonesboro at the "Tara Plantation," which used to be just Tara but now it's condos. She didn't want to be alone, since her fourth husband died. There's a big pool there—they fire up the Weber and "party." My mother uses "party" as a verb now. I'm really happy for her.

I had a coming-out party and all that, I admit it. But now I'm a performance artist. In my last piece I dressed up like a hoop-skirted antebellum beauty in an oxygen mask, and I had slide projections of Sherman tanks roll over me while I writhed in agony. People liked it.

Today I'm wandering around near Peachtree Center in kind of a fog, trying to find a Woolworth's that I took for granted my entire life but now it's as if it never existed. This kind of thing really rattles me.

All these New York—looking shoestores with maybe four pairs of incredibly chic shoes on display are opening. I need really ugly shower curtains for a new piece I'm writing, and now I don't know where to go.

All of a sudden I get the thought that the Gentrification of Atlanta is another Yankee scourge. I start to wonder if I could work this thought into my piece. Then I start to wonder if the thought is a smart, worthwhile thought. Then I start to wonder if I'm even slightly smart or interesting in the first place. Lately I've been thinking that if I had less hair people might take me

My boyfriend's name is Black—he's white. Scarlett and Black. I don't think I have to tell you how many stupid comments we get.

more seriously. Insecurity is my worst fault. "How can you possibly have the name Scarlett and be insecure?" my mother says. I think the genes are finally mutating.

Atlanta-bashing is the favorite hobby of most of my friends. They're always comparing everything to New York, even though New York is just a place you read about and feel inferior to, and no one in their right mind would ever want to actually live there. Not that my life here is so great. I live with my boyfriend in a decrepit studio apartment on Edgewood that's about the size and temperature of a pottery kiln. My boyfriend's name is Black—he's white. Scarlett and Black. I don't think I have to tell you how many stupid comments we get. He's never told me his real name, and I'm too shy to ask. He's a very talented bass player. There's a semiscene happening in Atlanta musically, and he's pretty well known. I mean, for here.

The thing is, he treats me like I'm just some kind of space junk, orbiting him. Faithfully and obsoletely. I did a piece where I tried to convey this with glass milk bottles and vinyl LP's going around a

Ken doll, but just for spite he said he didn't get it.

My only girlfriend that I honestly like, for deeper reasons than going to clubs, is Prissy. (Which is actually kind of weird, because I guess the original Scarlett had a slave named Prissy.) She's the head of an OB/GYN clinic, and she's black and very yuppie Achieving, but in an okay way. One time I got to be at a birth with her, for my girlfriend Melanie's baby that she had with artificial insemination from our friend Ashley, but that's another story. Anyway, Melanie was flipping out, and Prissy did

---

"Tomorrow's another day, Scarlett," Prissy says chirpily, and I get an unbelievable rush of déjà vu.

---

her Jive Slave act to crack us up: "Fo' Gawd, Miss Scarlett! Ah doan know nuthin' 'bout birthin' babies! We's got ter have a *doctah*! Preferably *white*! Preferably *male*!" She's a riot.

I'm meeting her at Mick's for a hamburger, and to help me figure out why I'm living with someone who ignores me.

"Why can't Black be more like Ashley?" I whine.

"Because Ashley's *gay*," Prissy says. "Wake up and smell the Fiesta Ware, babe. You have a great time with him and you love him and he listens to you and he has an incredible apartment because he's *gay*. Black will never, I guarantee you, be more like Ashley."

I've known Ashley Wilkes all my life. (Which is actually kind of weird, because I guess the original Scarlett knew a guy named Ashley.) He's the only man I've ever loved who has never once uttered a single comment that made me lie awake at night wondering what he meant. Of all the men who've loved me, this is a man I could marry. But Ashley likes boys like the honeybees like magnolias.

Suddenly I'm worried about my life.

"Prissy," I say, "I feel like I'm becoming a tragic figure."

Prissy grabs the check. People know I have money, and they know I know they know, but the thing they know best is how deeply a rich girl appreciates being allowed to feel poor. It's kind of pathetic, but there you have it.

"Tomorrow's another day, Scarlett," Prissy says chirpily, and I get an unbelievable rush of déjà vu.

I go home incredibly depressed. The heat is making me feel like I have the flu. For various reasons there happen to be five messages for me on the machine from male friends. Listening to one after another, even though what's said is totally innocent, it suddenly occurs to me that every one of them has kind of a crush on me. They're all a little jokey, a little cozy, the vowels lingered over. I'm not sure how this happened, or what I'm supposed to do about it. "Men have always loved me," says my mother, "and they'll always love you, too."

Big surprise: Black didn't shop. There's, like, a bottle of amaretto. I open the practically empty refrigerator and gaze into it as if I could magically turn the rancid butter into something good. There's a radish in the crisper drawer. One cruddy old radish. I gnaw on it like a hamster. A bead of sweat actually rolls down my back. And then, right there where I stand, I make a solemn vow.

As God is my witness, I'm moving out of this dump!

I want a nice husband, and a nice house, and nice things! And I can *afford* them!

I feel better already. "Fiddle-dee-dee!" I inexplicably laugh as I slam the refrigerator door. Maybe I'll get some cool clothes . . . visit long-lost Rhett in L.A. for a little while. (Which is actually kind of weird, because I guess the original Scarlett married a guy named Rhett.)

The thing about Atlanta is, when Pete falls out, you've always got Re-pete. ⏾

Southern Bellefleur

Tara, the main house, protrudes from the cankered land, an old bad tooth that won't come out by itself; with trees around it, a basement, that won't be pulled either; dominating, edificial.

In the campsite rental office, temporary, out back, Scarlett waits for Ashley to get back from city hall, the zoning committee meeting, the Historical Society hearings, that are supposed to determine whether Tara is historical or whether she can permanently subdivide it. While she waits Scarlett staples her hand, her fingers together, wanly, staples cracking the red nails, red coming up through the red shells, metal staples, Swingline.

Ashley enters the office, walking, with his feet, in shoes—leather, with socks under them, not under them actually, between them and his feet, over the feet, inside the shoes—and sits down. Speaking, Scarlett asks him how the meeting went.

It is hard to say, to describe, explain, elucidate, recount. The preservationists are cutting a bicycle path to the sea. Leaving everything standing in their wake. Not a patch of earth scorched, not a home razed to the ground in their wake. If Scarlett tries to have the building torn down they plan to condemn it and keep it preserved; this is the plan presented by eggheads at the newly established Vanderbilt

University Graduate School of Southern Studies. No, Tara will always belong to the O'Haras, Scarlett says.

To emphasize this point she hefts a tin wastebasket, oval, green, filled with scrap paper, food wrappers, pencil shavings, and clubs Ashley softly, slowly, dentingly, across the head with it.

Sometimes I don't know who is worse, Scarlett says: Do simple people, honest,

Yikes, Ashley says, I guess there is an undercurrent of violence, careless, mechanical, just beneath the veneer of day-to-day reality.

earnest, content, dreamless, demented, inbred, suck the worst or do the denizens of cross-disciplinary cultural history faculties, failed, impotent, barren, striving, disappointed?

Orally, Scarlett continues: My family, people who are related to each other, is going to lose all its money because Tara is the only, mysteriously, major building left standing in the South. The property, the house and real estate, owes taxes, money the government asks for, and it is clear I have to do something. My only choice is to subdivide and lease Tara in quarter-acre plots, tracts for trailers, homes, buildings for people to inhabit, live in, with their furniture, couches and chairs, dishes, inside —with them.

It's not fair anyhow to prohibit development now, after others have been permitted to do it, she sometimes feels, she says, after Seven Oaks was allowed to become the 7-O Industrial Park; a zoned plot for commercial structures; warehouses, factories—buildings for making things, other buildings for keeping things in, indoors, roofed.

This will be a good trailer park, she says, a place where people can put down roots, form tubers, send out tendrils, runners, shoots, suckers. Talking, with her voice, suddenly Scarlett pokes the receipts rod from her desk, the sharp long metal prongy thing with bills impaled on it, fluttering, the bills that is, into her ear, shallowly, never entering the ear canal damaging the drum, just around the rim. Yikes, Ashley says, I guess there is an undercurrent of violence, careless, mechanical, just beneath the veneer of day-to-day reality.

Then they're both quiet, the two of them, not admitting, somehow, that their dream may be stillborn.

Ashley walks, crestfallen, upset, racked, over to the Mr. Coffee machine, gleaming, steaming, aromatic, anachronistic, Mr. Coffee that is, not Ashley, and takes a cup, considers it, porcelain, hollowed, handled, impervious, for holding fluid in, and puts his face under the coffee spout instead. Feels the scalding, steaming hot coffee, mud, mocha, java, joe, imported, mountain grown, naturally decaffeinated to keep in that just-ground flavor and aroma, splashing into his eye sockets; burning through his lids, searing rods and cones in the retina, curdling the whites, like an egg. Then he sits down again.

On the wall a clock ticks once, round, with numbers painted on its face, for telling time, ticks again; and, a second later, again. ⏚

The Color Scarlett

Dear Aunt Pitty-Pat,
You know we O'Haras we have our pride. That is why it is so hurtful to be abducted and held captive here at the Radical Women's Army's Collective Hospice. Humiliate me though they try to they have locked me in the exact wrong place, in a utility closet and when they let me out they will see that I am proud and not broken because I still look flush as I am wearing a blouse I have made out of some shelving paper, skirt that is really a bath mat, that chafes, socks made out of manila envelopes. Shoes made out of bricks. A hat

made out of a soup tureen painted felt colored with creosote. One thing I have, that is my pride.

I am so frightened. I was lured here by a voice that seemed oddly familiar and I hear it now sometimes I call out Who is that Why are you holding me What is your name and it says Slug. Slug?

Mrs. _____ I am the leader here. Slug Overy is my name it says. But I know that voice It is familiar from somewhere I know I have heard it before.

Dear Aunt Pitty-Pat,
The Radical Women's Army's Collective Hospice is holding me for ransom. It makes me angry. That Slug Overy who is the leader seems haughty and distant and full of herself even if she is a good commander and everyone seems to do what she says and everyone in the cabal respects her very much I hate her and would like to cut her down to size.

Dear Aunt Pitty-Pat,
Slug comes to my cell yesterday.

Oh please let me go. Why are you holding me I say. Mrs. _____ we are holding you because if anyone has been kicked around by the patriarchy it is you. And if anyone is a prisoner of her sex it is you. And if we can re-educate you out of your gender-locked behaviors, out of your race-engendered bloodthirsty desire for real estate there is hope for anyone plus we're short on cash, hehehehe, and figure there must be someone who will pay to get you back. You just keep working on those ransom epistles.

All this time I am sitting for a portrait to go with the ransom epistle for everyone to know I am hostage. I am holding a copy of the 1889 Farmer's Almanac to prove when I am still alive. This is my own idea. I will teach that haughty Slug Overy a thing or two about ransom epistles. Slug Overy just mocks me though I think I could get her to accept me as an equal. Not that I care what she thinks. I hate her and that is all.

Dear Aunt Pitty-Pat,
Later I have another re-education talk with Slug Overy. I am mocking her but she can see that I am anxious to learn. She must see that. Oh what is coming over me?

I ask her why in the ransom epistle and elsewhere I am addressed as Mrs. _____. Is it to ironically symbolize race and gender-based cowed almost deific deference or to denote the tyrannical universality of my character, the oppressor or what?

Mrs. _____ I might do that to a name for all of those reasons Slug says but in your case you are Mrs. _____ because you have a different last name every time a body turns around.

That Slug toys with me and pretends boredom at my shenanigans.

But there is a sadness in Slug that the others cannot see and not only because she

---

I wasn't sure it was my turn to speak what without any quotation marks around or anything.

---

always has a bag over her head. Only I see it comes from because she has to be so hard. She needs someone to . . . someone to . . . ooh.

Dear Aunt Pitty-Pat,
Today Slug asks me what I had been doing to have fallen on such hard times before I came to the Collective. She asks me as a game to aid self-realization and is making me smoke reefer. I was a hardscrabble farmer I tell her.

Hardscrabble she asks me. I don't say anything. Then I catch on I'm sorry I say I just wasn't sure it was my turn to speak what without any quotation marks around or anything. What's a soul want scrabble for she asks me especially hardscrabble. What? Oh me again. I don't rightly know. Scrabble-pies. Scrabble-tarts. Scrabble-corn-cobbler. Scrabble-sauce. You know. Scrabble. Truth to tell I'm not really sure of what scrabble hard or otherwise looks like. I was dirt farming for a spell but grew disgruntled as I couldn't tell whether the new dirt was growing or was the same dirt as the day before. Then for a spell I was making carpetbags but again between you and me people don't as a rule have much use for carpetbags as most just carry carpets one place and that's home from the carpet store and then they just most usually don't move their carpets around at all.

I can tell that she is really truly very awfully interested in me. Mrs. _____ you are an idiot Slug says but with real compassion. My Lord! What are these feelings I'm feeling?

Dear Aunt Pitty-Pat,
No one has answered our ransom epistles. We have even tried composing them with the urgency of dialect. Yet there is no response from any of my suitors past or pres-

---

Mrs. _____ you are an idiot Slug says but with real compassion. My Lord! What are these feelings I'm feeling?

---

ent living or dead real or prospective or their heirs. We are both dispirited by this and smoke a lot of reefer and I suggest that we try as a last resort to ransom me to He.

Why do you call him He Slug says. I can tell Slug is excited because I have made some kind of breakthrough recognizing the uselessness of names in the context of naming the Constant Oppressor, and as a device He gives again that sense of quaking servitude that is so sought after in the epistolary form, especially when demanding money.

He Slug says?

That's his name. Lee He. He's from Canton. Came over to work for the Southern Pacific. After we try him what about trying Mr. _____?

What?

Mr. _____.

Who, him?

He?

Him, you know—_____.

Who?

Is it just Stockholm Syndrome or does Slug really care for me? I am so confused I don't even know which of us is talking. Yes, and neither do you, Slug says. Or if I'm thinking and you are listening. Then Slug is holding me for a long time in her strong arms or perhaps I'm holding her. Oh fiddledeewhee!

Sister Pitty-Pat,
The Goddess as my witness I have never been happier than today. More satisfied, if you catch my drift. I must tell Slug that. Since Slug must really love and trust me I know that. Sometimes I feel so lost though so liberated. Like a beauty with a beast only more correct sexually politically-wise. So now I must confront Slug.

Slug Overy I say I know who you are now You don't have to hide. I have discovered the strength in my womanhood as you have and as equals you can show me your face now I know that you are who I once called Prissy.

Prissy? Slug says. Scarlett, it's me . . . Ashley. ∎

The #1 #1 Bestseller

DIURETICS

The Modern Science of Purification

W.C. HUBBARD

Founder of The Church of Urology

DIURETICS

No one has ever followed Dianetics guru L. Ron Hubbard more consistently—or more literally—than W. C. Hubbard (no relation), author of the best-selling genitourinary tract *Diuretics* and founder of the Church of Urology, whose adherents measure the purity of their bodies using electronic devices, call P-meters, sold to them at generous discounts by W.C.'s own philanthropic foundation.

A major factor in the success of *Diuretics* was a dramatic TV spot demonstrating that the book could answer even the most troubling questions of those who had "struggled in vain for purification." Sample copy:

Why is it you can drink beer for two hours without having to go, and then you go, and five minutes later you have to go again? Page 25

What is it about asparagus? Page 133

If you hiccup and sneeze at the same time while taking a whiz, do you have a heart attack or disappear into into the fifth dimension, or what? Page 261.

FIRST COMMUNION

FIRST COMMUNION

Whitley Strieber's experiences of contact with extraterrestrial beings were so bizarre he could hardly even believe them himself. Scout's honor. And the experience of sharing these experiences in his best-selling book *Communion* was so exhausting and traumatic he could barely bring himself to write a sequel at all. Really. But lucky for us, he did gamely submit to hypnosis one more time, and recalled an alien visitation even more fantastic than the others. The creatures appeared in a flying collection plate, led Strieber to an abandoned monastery, and made their demand...

AN HONEST TO GOD TRUE STORY

A

STEPHEN KING

BOOK-OF-THE-WEEK CLUB
SEQUEL

Pet Seminary

HOLY TERRIERS

SEQUELS FROM THE STEPHEN KING BOOK-OF-THE-WEEK CLUB

One of the important publishing stories of 1990 was the much-ballyhooed launch of the Stephen King Book-of-the-Week Club, whose ads featured the tireless master of the macabre's personal guarantee that members would receive "a brand-new follow-up to one of my famous works every single Monday for as long as you continue to subscribe."

A

STEPHEN KING

BOOK-OF-THE-WEEK CLUB
SEQUEL

Pujo

The car that chases dogs

In addition to the blockbusters pictured here, early Book-of-the-Week Club selections included *The Jerry Builders*, about ethereal creatures with the power to induce building code violations; a pair of sequels to *The Shining—The Buffing* and *The Waxing*; and a fifteen-book series of *Carrie* spinoffs, including *Carry On, Carrie*; *The Carry-On Carrie*; *Carrion Carrie*; and *Sister Carrie's Sister, Carrie*, which also achieved success as a quickie television movie.

PRIDE AND EXTREME PREJUDICE

The action-packed sequel to *Pride and Prejudice* introduced a new Bennet sister, "Dirty" Harriet, who won the hearts of Jane Austen fans by forestalling an insult from Elizabeth Bennet's old nemesis, Lady Catherine de Bourgh, with a cool "I have no objection, your ladyship, to your proceeding, since, by so doing, you shall render my afternoon quite agreeable."

AMERICAN · SEQUEL SOCIETY · II

vegetable farm

He wants to take over.

They couldn't care less.

• AN AMERICAN SEQUEL SOCIETY CLASSIC • AN AMERICAN SEQUEL SOCIETY CLASSIC • AN AMERICAN

Pride and Extreme Prejudice

"A MAGNUM OPUS."
—*Books and Ammo*

VEGETABLE FARM

With its storybook simplicity and barnyard setting, George Orwell's *Animal Farm* was perhaps the slyest allegorical tale of human prejudice and political corruption ever written. *Vegetable Farm*, a sequel completed just before Orwell's death in 1950, conveys a very different message. Do you recognize this carrot? Orwell seems to ask. Are we ourselves the apathetic romaine, the dispassionate kohlrabi, the stupefied potatoes unmindful of the threat of a newly malevolent tuber? Or is everything just going to be okay? Or what?

SOLITUDE: THE NEXT ONE HUNDRED YEARS

THE FALL OF THE PATRIARCH

"SOMETIMES TRUTH IS STRANGER THAN MAGICAL FICTION." *PANAMA TIMES*

🏛 LA SOCIEDAD AMERICANA DE SECUELAS

Marquez implied in the final chapter of his One Hundred Years of Solitude *that there were no survivors of the destruction of Macondo, but Nigromanta the Prostitute, unaware that she was pregnant with Aureliano's daughter, did escape.*

THE GENEALOGY OF *SOLITUDE*

José Arcadio Buendía
m. Úrsula Iguarán

|

José Arcadio
m. Rebeca

|

Arcadio
(by Pilar Ternera)
m. S. Sofía de la Piedad

|

Aureliano Segundo
m. Fernanda del Carpio

|

Renata Remedios (Meme)

|

Aureliano
(by Mauricio Babilonia)

|

Maria Moreno
(by Nigromanta)

|

General Antonio Noriega
(by Ricuarte Noriega)

The village of Macondo, the setting of Gabriel García Marquez's One Hundred Years of Solitude, *was located in northern Colombia, but in 1903, shortly after Macondo was destroyed by a great hurricane, the land on which it had stood became part of the new Republic of Panama. It was there that José Arcadio Buendía's great-great-great-great granddaughter gave birth to his great-great-great-great-great grandson, Manuel Antonio Noriega.*

Solitude: The Next One Hundred Years

Many years later, as he faced the yanquí soldiers in the street outside the Papal Nuncio's house, General Antonio Noriega was to remember that distant afternoon when his adoptive mother took him to see the Canal. For a dollar apiece, they traveled from Panama City to Colón and back again on the railroad, and Luísa Sánchez pointed out to the serious boy with the deeply pitted face the great Miraflores Locks, the vast Gatun Lake, the stupendous excavation of the Gaillard Cut, and the long line of ships from every place in the world being lifted up and lowered down the amazing stairs of water. Antonio Noriega looked at the ships, which had the names of foreign ports painted on their sterns but flew the flag of Panama, and the buildings in the Zone, which were in Panama but flew the flag of the United States. "Is there anything in this country that is not for sale?" he asked.

What Luísa Sánchez wished to say was that No, there was nothing that was not for sale, but the year before, the United Fruit Company, seeking to end once and for all the vocal but ineffectual opposition of the banana workers to its plans to cut wages, had bought all the ways there were of saying "no," and so she shrugged her shoulders and said the only thing she could think of, which was "noodle."

When the Americans first recruited General Antonio Noriega to be a spy for them, he was still only a cadet at the Chorrillos Military Academy in Peru. A man who called himself Señor Bruno and who would not let anyone call him Mr. Brown, even though he spoke no Spanish and Brown was not his real name anyway, gave him five dollars a month for the names of students who displayed communist sympathies. Antonio Noriega asked what would be done to the people he informed

---

"Is there anything in this country that is not for sale?" Antonio Noriega asked.

---

on. Señor Bruno looked grave. "They will never again receive the correct change from any soft-drink vending machine anywhere in the Free World," he said.

Later, General Antonio Noriega was able to spot leftists by the thick calluses on their palms where they had repeatedly struck the hard metal panels of the automatic dispensers of sodas and colas, and the scarred toes of their shoes where they had kicked the heavy metal cabinets in impotent fury.

General Omar Torrijos had become ruler of Panama because the gypsy fortune-teller, Exasperación Amanita, had mixed up his cards, which foretold his future as the ringleader of the Circus Espectacular de Panama, with the cards of Simón Bolívar Torrentes, who now drilled the sleepy lions and temperamental elephants with the dedication and precision of a born leader.

Since General Omar Torrijos had no particular aptitude for running a government, other than a great talent for showmanship, he left the business of the state to Colonel Antonio Noriega, who as a result

---

George Bush's hands jumped around like rabbits when he spoke, and it was not words that came out of his mouth, but tiny pieces of candy.

---

soon became the most powerful man in Panama, instead of being killed in a bar by the pimp of a prostitute he had beaten, which was his true destiny. The man who received in his place the fatal knife thrust, a drunken communist named Gromyko Sánchez, thus died without accomplishing the act which fate had ordained for him, which was to shoot the American Vice-President George Bush in the Panama City airport in December of 1983.

In another December, in the year when the United States of America were two hundred years old, Colonel Antonio Noriega went to Washington to meet George Bush. This was just after he had set off the car bombs in the Canal Zone as General Omar Torrijos had ordered because the Treaty Talks had broken down. Everyone expected that the yanquís would be angry, and Colonel Antonio Noriega had prepared himself for threats, accusations, and ultimatums. He was ready to explain that the explosions were in fact spontaneous, a result of the hidden passions that lay so close to the surface in the tropics. An old station wagon, jealous when its owner thoughtlessly leaves colored brochures advertising a sporty new model on its seats, detonates from pure rage. These things happened in a place like Panama.

But when George Bush entered the dark, cool room in the Panamanian Embassy, Colonel Antonio Noriega knew at once that there would be no need for apologies or excuses. Bush's hands jumped around like rabbits when he spoke, and it was not words that came out of his mouth, but tiny pieces of candy: gumdrops, chocolate kisses, horehound drops, bits of taffy, tiny squares of fudge, little round mints, strips of brightly colored ribbon candy, loops of red and black licorice, soft cubes of caramel, jellybeans, sourballs, jujubes, fragments of peanut brittle, and mocha swirls with cordial centers. They dropped on the silk-covered sofa, on the marble coffeetable, and on the Aubusson carpet, and an aide quickly picked them up and put them in little plastic bags, which he placed in a large black attaché case.

After Bush had left, Colonel Antonio Noriega asked the Ambassador what Bush had said, but they did not know the meaning of the only word he had spoken that either one of them could remember: "Gosharoonie."

When the plane of General Omar Torrijos crashed into the mountain, it was because it had become tired of flying, just as the General had become tired of ruling, having caught the terrible disease of weariness from the Shah of Iran, whom he had allowed to come to Panama. While the fatigued dictator lived in solitude on the island of Contádora, the ocean became so tired that the tides and waves ceased entirely, the fish snored like old men, and along the beaches the leaves of the palm trees drooped to the ground like the feathers of gigantic sleeping parrots.

In the same year that General Omar Torrijos died, the Movie Actor became President of the United States. Colonel Antonio Noriega sent away for all his films and watched them again and again. He began to swagger. He briefly grew a mustache. He ordered a black uniform. He stopped using the Swiss creams on his acne-scarred face. He started smoking long, thin cigars.

His comrade, Colonel Rubén Darío Paredes, whom he would later betray as he betrayed everyone, asked him what was on his mind.

"I now know for certain what my destiny is," said Colonel Antonio Noriega with both pride and sadness. "I am to be the Bad Guy."

O n the day before he was promoted to General and became Comandante of the National Guard, Colonel Antonio Noriega paid a visit to Ivan Trilha, the Brazilian sorcerer, and asked him to look at the cards. The *brujo* shuffled the deck and laid out the hand. His voice turned solemn. "I see great misfortune ahead for a powerful, secretive Colonel with millions in drug money who has sold arms to murderous bandits, caused the deaths of hundreds of innocent people, and is the mastermind of vast intrigues in a corrupt, undemocratic, and brutal country which has a vain old fool as a puppet President." Colonel Antonio Noriega's rough face turned ashen. The cards never lied.

"Whoa, hold the phone," said Ivan Trilha suddenly. "It isn't you. It's some gringo named North."

E ach of the airplanes belonging to Pablo Escobar had been furnished in the style of a particular epoch which the Colombian drug seller, who read only history books and bartenders' guides, had found significant. The one in which General Antonio Noriega flew to Medellín had a cabin that was a replica of the Hall of Mirrors at Versailles, and the crystal pendants on the chandeliers tinkled as the plane bounced in the turbulent tropical air. He sat in a Louis XIV chair in the middle of the vast glass-lined fuselage, eating with gold utensils off Sèvres porcelain on a little ormolu table that folded down from the damask back of the gilded chair in front of him. The meal was overcooked veal parmigiana with wax beans and au gratin potatoes, with a hot salad and a melted jellied ice-cream cake dessert, for even the Drug Cartel, with all its power, could not make airplane food tolerable.

Pablo Escobar drove him in a black Mercedes to his ranch with the zoo with over a hundred animals. They sat in a simple adobe room in the old colonial building and drank Rob Roys, sidecars, and gimlets. As they talked, money began seeping under the door and gathering in heaps on the polished tile floors like wind-blown leaves. The casement windows swung open, and a solid mass of twenty, fifty, and one-hundred dollar bills spilled into the room, filling the air with the heavy leaded scent of the indelible inks used by the American mint.

Pablo Escobar led General Antonio Noriega up a narrow wooden ladder and

The casement windows swung open, and a solid mass of twenty, fifty, and one-hundred dollar bills spilled into the room...

through a trapdoor to the wide, flat roof from which they could see the long, green waves of currency boiling down the hill and flowing around the old stone building with a dry, fluttering noise like millions of bats swirling out of a cave. "You see the problem," said Pablo Escobar.

T he drug sellers wished to ship their drugs through Panama and to build a processing plant in the jungle near the border with Colombia, but before he would permit them to do so, General Antonio Noriega went once again to see Ivan Trilha, the Brazilian *brujo,* to consult the spirits. It was one thing to accept payment from the drug sellers to save them from drowning in the tidal wave of dollars by helping to channel the immense river of cash through the banks of Panama, but to become involved with the drugs themselves was a dangerous step.

"You are right, my friend," said Ivan Trilha, reading the cards. "The spirits are indeed angry with a huge, immoral cartel that is making billions of dollars by selling a white powder that has brought poverty, sickness, and death to hundreds of thousands of people."

"Cocaine," said General Antonio Noriega, "the Medellín drug sellers."

"Nah," said Ivan Trilha, "infant formula. The multinational corporations have been selling it in Latin America for years. Very bad stuff."

General Antonio Noriega's uneven face brightened. "What goes around comes around," he said happily.

"Hey, this just in," said Trilha, examining another card. "Have you ever heard of an island called Grenada?"

Because of its exceptional solitude, the place where the town of Macondo had stood many years earlier had been chosen by the drug sellers as the site of their cocaine factory. The great wind that in 1903

"Hey, this just in," said Trilha, examining another card. "Have you ever heard of an island called Grenada?"

---

had utterly erased all traces of the settlement and made the sailors on the cruiser U.S.S. *Nashville* seasick as they sailed to Cristobal to separate Panama from Colombia had deposited a thick layer of red soil blown all the way from Africa, and now a dense, wet forest covered the invis-

ible streets of Macondo, and the dark rows of trunks were only occasionally broken by the twisted shape of one of the immortal almond trees.

The ghosts of José Arcadio Buendía and Melquíades the gypsy came to see the strange installation and to examine the vats and racks and pipes and generators and powerful floodlights and the raised timber walkways.

"They have found gold," said José Arcadio Buendía. "I always knew it was around here somewhere."

"No, my friend," said Melquíades, "This is a plant for processing many tons of cocaine to sell to the gringos."

José Arcadio Buendía remembered the numbing powder the barber in Macondo had packed into his gums before he had extracted his ancient, decayed molars.

"The gringos must have terrible teeth," he said. "That is surely why they are so crazy for bananas. It's obviously the only thing they can eat. And it is their awful toothaches that make them so amazingly mean," he concluded, with considerable satisfaction at this deduction.

Melquíades opened his mouth to counter this perfectly sensible theory with the completely implausible facts, but as soon as he began to speak, his words were lost in the hammering racket of Panamanian National Guard helicopters circling to land in the clearing, because General Antonio Noriega had betrayed the drug sellers, as he betrayed everyone.

Fidel Castro did not want a war between the drug sellers and the Panamanians because Panama was useful to him as it was useful to everyone, and so he asked General Antonio Noriega to come to Cuba. They met in the Palace of the Revolution, and Fidel Castro took General Antonio Noriega to see a few of the items from his collection of lethal devices used in the 714 attempts on his life by the CIA.

"If you don't make peace with the Cartel, they'll just hire someone to murder you," he said, showing, one by one, the booby-trapped Spanish-language Scrabble game, the flammable barbecue apron, the croquet set with the exploding balls, the lava lamp filled with napalm, and the radioactive mood ring.

"You simply have no idea what a pain in the ass it is to have people trying to kill you all the time," said Fidel Castro.

After he made peace with the Cartel, it was impossible even for General Antonio Noriega, who forgot nothing and had a file on everyone, to keep track of all the plane flights from the tiny jungle airstrips with landing lights made from pots of flaming oil. The pilots, all of whom worked for one of the 26 airlines owned by the CIA, also became confused. As a result, when a Contra guerrilla pushed the plunger on what he thought was a bomb that would blow up an oil refinery in Managua, he set off an electric spark in a parcel containing 118 kilos of pure cocaine, and on the streets of Detroit, 47 people died of overdoses from a Czech rocket propellant intended for bazooka shells for a right-wing death squad in El Salvador.

The Drug Enforcement Administration officers on assignment in Panama became so demoralized by the fact that everyone they discovered dealing in drugs was working for some other agency of the U.S. government that they gave up and spent their days at the beach, teaching the drug-sniffing dogs to catch Frisbees.

Not long after General Antonio Noriega arranged for the death of Dr. Hugo Spadafora, the Perpetual Revolutionist, and fired the first of the Musical Presidents, Mr. William Casey asked him to come to Washington to see him. It was always difficult to talk with Mr. Casey because the CIA Director had lost entirely the ability to tell the truth. This incapacity made it very hard for his subordinates to respond to his wishes unless they were expressed as a yes or no answer to a question, in which case they could simply do the opposite of what had been ordered. But when

Mr. Casey asked for a certain file to be brought, what did he really want? A cup of coffee? Satellite photographs of Estonia? A pocket comb? An Irish diplomatic passport? A shoeshine?

"Excuse me for not getting up," said Mr. Casey as he rose and strode across the room to shake the hand of General Antonio Noriega. "The old artificial leg is bothering me again," he confided, tapping the healthy flesh of his perfectly normal left knee.

They sat on a sofa in the corner of the office, sidestepping a crew of CIA workmen with paintchips and fabric swatches who had interpreted an order by the Director to blow up an office building in Beirut as a request to redecorate his office. The previous week, his demand for a harmonica had led to the kidnapping of a labor leader in the Philippines.

"You know, General," said Mr. Casey, "the U.S. government never condones any criminal acts whatsoever, regardless of the desirability of the ends. The struggle against communism must always be waged fully within the law." He paused. "Here, have a cigar," he said, handing General Antonio Noriega his desk clock.

The last time General Antonio Noriega met with Colonel Oliver North was in London just before the Movie Actor fired

---

It was always very hard to talk with Mr. Casey because the CIA Director had lost entirely the ability to tell the truth.

---

him. They walked together through the big park across the street from the hotel where they were both staying. Neither of them wore a uniform, but Colonel Oliver North looked so much like a soldier and the poses he was always striking were so military that the pigeons came by the dozens and sat on his head and his shoulders and even on his arms as he made his stiff, solemn gestures. Finally the two officers had to go back to the hotel and have North's suit cleaned.

They sat in General Antonio Noriega's room, drinking bourbon, and Colonel Oliver North explained his plan to disgrace the entire Sandinista leadership in the eyes of their people by kidnapping the top Comandantes and making them appear on the television show "Hollywood Squares."

"Why don't you just assassinate them?" asked General Antonio Noriega.

Colonel Oliver North smiled his strange smile, but he was clearly offended. "It's not the American way," he said firmly.

Although the Americans did not try to assassinate General Antonio Noriega as they had tried to assassinate Fidel Castro, they tried everything else to get rid of him. They indicted him. They threatened him. They offered him bribes to leave, and

---

Although the Americans did not try to assassinate Antonio Noriega as they had tried to assassinate Fidel Castro, they tried everything else to get rid of him.

---

when he would not accept them, they launched countless plots against him. In Operation Fancy Tonnage, they forged an order for 60,000 frozen pizzas from a company in New Jersey and had them shipped to Panama and delivered in a refrigerated container to his headquarters in the Comandancia. In Operation Cruel Snooze, they short-sheeted every bed in the barracks of his elite Brigade 2000. In Operation Snazzy Tassel, they used sophisticated Blackhawk helicopters to paper his hacienda with nearly four miles

of toilet tissue.

General Antonio Noriega stood by the window in the Comandancia and looked out at the lights of the Canal. The silence was broken now and then by the wet impact of the water bombs dropping from the American stealth planes circling 70,000 feet over Panama City in Operation Damp Anvil. General Antonio Noriega thought of all the deals the yanquís had proposed and that he had turned down.

"How on earth did I become the last thing in Panama not for sale?" he asked himself in wonderment.

Many months later, after the Americans sent 20,000 armed men to arrest him, General Antonio Noriega sat in the little cell in Miami, reading the long indictment that accused him of crimes that carried a penalty of 145 years in prison—with good behavior, perhaps one hundred years of solitude. He looked at the steel bars of the cell and he thought of the other barred doors in the vaults of the sixteen banks in Switzerland that held the sixteen separate, identical, meticulously detailed copies of his memoirs, the amazing tale of death and drugs and money and guns that intertwined so magically with the lives of the Movie Actor, and the Man with the Hands Like Rabbits, and Colonel Oliver North, and Mr. Casey, and all the generals, and diplomats, and bankers, and spies. He recalled all of the remarkable incidents that everyone had thought were wiped out, erased, shredded, and exiled from the memory of men, and although he was a man condemned to one hundred years of solitude, General Antonio Noriega's stupendously ugly face bore a beatific smile. ⌀

Niccola Machiavelli's
The Princess

Little is known about Niccolò Machiavelli's wife, Niccola, but these excerpts from the sequel she wrote to his famous treatise on politics and government, The Prince, *show that she was more than a match for her celebrated husband, both as a prose stylist and as a cynical observer of human nature.*

The Various Kinds of Relationship Which the Princess May Enter Into and the Ways in Which They May Be Instituted

All relationships through which women may hold sway over men are either informal liaisons or formal marriages. I will not here speak of informal liaisons, except insofar as they are a necessary and temporary prelude to the forging of more permanent and lasting bonds, for the Princess who uses her head for any other purpose than as a place to store her crown knows that a form of cohabitation that can be terminated without her consent, that does not require the intervention of a sympathetic court, and that leaves the determination of the amount of a cash settlement to the largesse of a lover whose ardor has cooled, is something to be avoided as if it were the very Plague itself.

I will therefore deal only with formal marriages, which may have as their object either a man who, previous to his wedding, lived according to his own desires, or one who has through a prior marriage become accustomed to the rule of another Princess. In either instance, the husband chosen by the Princess may be acquired by her through the exercise of craft and subterfuge, or else he may fall in love with her of his own accord, in which case the Princess, after a suitable delay calculated to disguise the preexistence of her nuptial intentions, allows herself to be conquered by the very object of her plans of conquest. In both instances, when the marriage is terminated, which may be by mutual consent or as the result of a complaint brought by one or the other based upon a real or an imagined grievance, the Princess, by virtue of her clear legal status, will be in a position to perform one last wifely duty, namely, to take the Prince by the most direct route possible to the place where the cleaners dwell.

Of the Art of Conversation, and Why the Princess Who Wishes to Impress a Man with Her Eloquence Ought to Remain Silent

When the Princess seeks to demonstrate to a man that she is well-spoken, she should on no account attempt to do so through the faculty of speech, for if there is one thing that men prefer to hear above all else, excepting only the plaudits of an approving crowd, it is the sound of their own voices. Thus, the Princess who is disposed to permit any man to talk at length without interruption on whatever subject he may choose will be adjudged a good conversationalist even if she has the intellect of a garden shrub, whereas if she interjects observations of her own, other than simple affirmations or expressions of awe and amusement, even if they be examples of great feats of learning or of rhetorical skill, she will be regarded as a nuisance and a vixen. And while it cannot be denied that the Princess may find it difficult to hold her tongue over long periods of time, she has only to content herself with the certain knowledge that once the marriage vows are irrevocably sealed, her husband is going to have need of a mason's tools to insert so much as a single word into the solid, unbroken wall of her discourse.

Of Pre-Nuptial Agreements

Although the Princess should always assure the Prince that it is his charms and not his wealth or situation that attract her to him, she should never consent to a practical demonstration of this assertion in the form of a contract limiting her claims upon his estate in the event of a divorce, for no matter how generous the prospective settlement may be, it will always amount to much less than can be obtained from a jury trial or extorted through threats of litigation. If the object of her matrimonial interest should press her upon this matter, the Princess should immediately protest with great sorrow and indignation that she is being treated as little better than a prostitute. It is a rare man who, when confronted with this accusation, will perceive that a business-like compact with a professional consort would, in fact, be a far more prudent course of action than the one he is about to embark upon, or that he is poised to enter into precisely such an arrangement with a gifted amateur without having first agreed upon the price.

Why the Princess, Once Wed, Should Contrive Without Delay to Become Pregnant

Regardless of any agreements she may have made with the Prince on the subject of when or whether to have children, the Princess, beginning on her wedding night, must apply her undivided attention and the totality of her womanly skills to the task of conceiving a child, taking advantage of the Prince's inevitable bafflement on matters regarding the inner workings of her anatomy to effect the process of impregnation without his active cooperation or knowledge if necessary. The imperative urgency of the matter is based upon a simple if melancholy fact: In the eyes of every juror who will ever sit to consider a bill of divorcement, there are but two images of a woman: The Harlot and The Madonna, the first being any childless woman who is not yet completely a crone, the second being any woman who has a child, even if she possesses the alluring beauty of Aphrodite. A married woman without progeny may well win the jury's admiring glances, but rarely their sympathy, and in awarding her a sum of alimony, they will invariably think in terms of the amounts appropriate to the payment of a prostitute, the value of whose time is set by convention. But were this same jury to regard the identical woman in the company of her children, they would not see a courtesan whose embraces they might think of sharing, but rather the image of their own mothers whom they would die to protect from any who might harbor those very thoughts and to whom they would gladly give all the gold in the world, or, so generous an award not being within their power, at the very least all the gold in the possession of the Prince.

The Way to Dominate a Man Who, Previous to Being Married, Lived According to His Own Desires

If the Princess marries a man who has been married before, she will find him accustomed to the subjugation of a wife and need only substitute her usages and commands for those of her divorced or deceased predecessor. But if the Prince has heretofore lived in a state of bachelorhood, and is used to liberty, the Princess must begin on the very day following the wedding the work of destroying his former way of life and imposing her rule.

To accomplish this end, she should declare at once that whatever lodgings he may occupy, no matter how sumptuous or well-appointed, are of insufficient grandeur for their joint habitation and she should select the accommodations that will replace them. She should then take in hand the decoration of their new apartments, ensuring that while their overall aspect is pleasing, there is nonetheless no single chamber among them in which the Prince feels wholly comfortable. She should further see to it that there are no rooms in which masculine pursuits, such as card-playing, billiards, or the like, can be carried on without considerable discomfort, owing to the absence of light, the awkwardness of the space, the inappropriateness of the furnishings, or the general inhospitality of the surroundings.

The Princess should next convince the Prince to change whatever style of clothing he has been accustomed to wear to another less suitable to him, and persuade him as well to take up new hobbies, interests, and pursuits and to forsake those which had formerly engaged his attention. And when the friends of his former unwed life make gentle fun at these transformations, she should take every opportunity to remind the Prince of these harmless remarks, converting them through repetition and exaggeration into cruel and unjustified insults to his person, and thereby gradually secure the banishment of these long-time comrades from his side on the grounds of rude behavior. Once she has arranged their removal from his affections, she may replace them with trustworthy companions from her own circle, who may be relied upon to report to her in confidence on all the Prince's activities and to take her part in any disputes that may occur. Only when she has accomplished all these things may the Princess be truly said to have gained ascendancy in her own household.

Why Tears Are a More Effective Response to an Affront than the Aerial Dispatch of Crockery

If the Princess takes offense at some action or remark of the Prince, she should not seek an immediate redress of the insult by throwing dishware at him, for if she misses, she will look ridiculous, and if she succeeds in doing him an injury, no matter how satisfying this may be to her, it will cause him but slight pain for a brief period; and further it will permit the Prince to judge himself to be the aggrieved party and to present himself in that role to others, displaying his bruise as proof of the Princess' way-

ward nature. If, on the other hand, the Princess contains her anger and responds with copious tears, then once the Prince's temper has abated, he will blame himself for his meanness and will wound himself many times over with the memory of his incivility and thereby suffer a far greater hurt over a much longer time than any that could be inflicted by the impact of a dish, even if it were hurled by Athena herself. And the Princess will be able, on countless future occasions, to remind him of his discourtesy and thereby obtain for herself costly gifts to assuage the great distress she will claim to feel at her recollection of the indignity she endured at his hands.

Why the Princess Should Encourage the Prince to Confess to Her His Past Misdeeds, and Then Once He Does So, in Spite of Having Pledged to Be of a Forgiving Nature, Instead Come Down Upon His Head Like an Hundredweight of Roofing-tiles

As soon following the marriage ceremony as the opportunity presents itself, the Princess should, by means of sweet words and assurances of understanding and forgiveness, prevail upon the Prince to reveal to her his past amorous history in the name of furthering the trust between them by making all of their secrets as open to each other as their hearts themselves. When at last the Prince, moved by her professions of love and his own male pride, consents to divulge the details of his youthful escapades, the Princess should attend to his recital in stony silence, and then, when he has finished, fly into an inconsolable fury at the proof, offered from his very lips, of his wanton conduct. She should accuse him of every vice she can think of, from vile carnality to the venal sin of lust, not failing in her tirade to reprove herself for her singular lack of judgment in having formed a holy union with a lecher and a reprobate.

If the Prince should remind her of her promise to pardon all, she should say that she will indeed endeavor to forgive his abominable debauchery and turpitude, but that it is not in her power ever to forget them. At this, the Prince will feel not only mortifying shame at his conduct, but also bitter frustration at his own idiocy in having provided evidence against himself, and upon these twin pillars of his sense of disgrace and his feeling of foolishness, the Princess will begin to lay the firm foundations of a secure and prosperous marriage. ⚏

Finn Fin

Late in 1989, a graduate student of the University of Heidelberg, combing the sacred scribblings of James Joyce in an effort to establish the supreme significance (or utter absurdity) of a shockingly deleted (or positively nonexistent) semicolon (page 237, line 4) in the very latest Definitive Edition of Ulysses, *made a truly startling discovery: the hitherto unsuspected final page of* Finnegans Wake.

Generations of PhDs have assumed that Joyce's cryptic masterpiece concludes with the words, "A way a lone a last a loved a long the"—a sentence fragment designed to send the reader, the narrator and that somnolent Finn, Mr. H.C. Earwicker, back (eternally) to the opening lines of the work. Yet this newfound text appears to establish that Joyce considered, but then abandoned, this sophomoric device, preferring in the end a more traditional denouement.

riverrun, past Eve and Adam's, from swerve of shore to bend of Hey! Wade a secant! Halt yer hearses! Woe there! Schtopp! Tell the writher we scene this park all ready! Didja view displace afore? Wail, I can't praise the phrase, but the nimbus familia. Ah, now eye memember! Tis the opening loins agen, all backtofront! Thesis beginnegan! Sum kinder jerk? Legpull? Gag? Sing a round, and aroun vicco! A cosmical egg's it? Whirled witout end? As the oul' woman said when her bike up an bitter, it's a vicious cycle! A roundhouse, right? Give us a brakeman! Loan us a fin.

Listen, Timebalm. Clickclock tictalk, hick(haec)hock, mickmock BRINGA-RINGATINGLING! Wutzit? A morning eruction? Bellzahell? Plural belles? Alarm cock growing! Whackit, ya daughterin' oldman! Donne!

Jim revised, see Howth here Isis, Finn against reason from the bad! Pissanthropos directus. Follow yer knows to Java, man. Waycup and smile the coffin: Hot Cuppa an' Eggs! Up an atom! Eurup!

Mr. Humphrey Earwicker, publican, sat up in his bed, smacked his lips, farted solemnly, stretched, yawned.

"Oh, I've had such a curious dream!" said Humphrey, and so he got up and ran off, thinking while he ran, as well he might, what a wonderful dream it had been.

THE END

The Way Things Break

On the opposite page is the $3.00 umbrella, one of the dozens of failsure items illustrated in *The Way Things Break*. Others include the luggage zipper, drugstore pantyhose, and the B-1 bomber.

Leonard Bergner, a management consultant en route from Dallas-Fort Worth to Boston, was inspired to write this sequel when, as he scrambled to board a connecting flight after his crippled 747 had been redirected to Salt Lake City, his briefcase popped open and his copy of David Macaulay's The Way Things Work *was mangled in an airline security conveyor belt.*

THE WAY THINGS BREAK

THE $3.00 UMBRELLA

A $3.00 umbrella can be broken in a number of ways, defying the laws of physics by demonstrating that a simple action may in fact have an unequal and randomly adverse reaction. The explanation for the umbrella's amazing fragility lies in its poor construction. A breeze, gravity, the natural moisture of a palm — any of these is more than sufficient to cause its handle to fly off and its skeleton to contort into characteristic shapelessness.

A disposable nylon sleeve prevents the $3.00 umbrella from malfunctioning prematurely. Once this has been removed, the operator unsnaps a safety tab, aims the umbrella sideways, and a feeble spring action expands the canopy into a small, flaccid arc. The umbrella is then raised to an upright position over the head: it provides adequate shelter for a distance of up to fifty yards, then breaks.

LOOSE FABRIC
Nylon fabric is rendered useless as protection against the rain.

IMPAIRED COLLAPSIBILITY
Shaft fails to perform expected telescoping action.

BROKEN BUTTON
Remains depressed when pushed.

METAL FATIGUE
Shaft shears at the handle after repeated attempts at closure.

EXPOSED SPOKE
Single thread holding the fabric breaks, revealing spoke.

1. OPENING
User attempts to open umbrella in driving rain . . .

2. GUST OF WIND
Umbrella is blown inside out. Arrow shows direction of wind.

3. TRASHCAN
User disposes of broken umbrella.

While on a visit to the Lübeck *Sommerkomödiefest* in 1503, the early Renaissance painter and engraver Albrecht Dürer attended a stock company production of *Sir Gawain and the Green Knight at the Opera*, which was first staged in England in 1382 and immediately became an annual fixture at the international humor fair held in northern Germany each July. So impressed was Dürer that, before leaving Lübeck, he created this steel engraving of the play's most memorable bit of comic business: a slapstick joust between Sir Gawain and Sir Bercilak, the notorious Green Knight.

Sir Gawain and the Green Knight at the Opera

This ironic follow-up to the medieval epic poem Sir Gawain and the Green Knight *may well be the first comedy sketch ever written in the English language, although such assertions are virtually impossible to prove with absolute certainty. What is beyond dispute, however, is the magnitude of the influence this fragment of dramatic farce—commonly known to Middle English scholars as "The Gawayne Sequelle"—has had on American vaudeville, and it remains as fresh and surprising today as it was when it was first written over 600 years ago.*

ENTER SOLUS ye GREENE KNYGHTE
He fteppeth on ye fkynne of a peeld froote,[1] *and falleth on hys bomme.*

GREENE KNYGHTE
Nay, butte I longe to telle ye. Yester nicht I hadde y-doffen myne armore and mayde me reddy for to sleepen, whan that I horde a sownde withoot, a grate noyse and rorynge. Seezed I mye trvfty fworde, and ranne to battel. And I flew a myghtee dragon in mye finglette. Howe that he gotte hym in mye finglette, I shalle neer knowe.
A voyce cryeth fromme ye thronge: Telle vs a merrye jaype!

GREENE KNYGHTE
Verrylye, thyse *are* ye merrye jaypes!

From ye wynges, a pye[2] *flyeth throwghe ye ayre, and fmiteth hym fvlle in ye fayce.*
EXIT, ye KNYGHTE, *to mvckle loffter*
ENTER at feveral doores, SIR GAWAYNE *and* KYNGE ARTHVR

SIR GAWAYNE
Welle mette, Kynge Arthvr. Nay, bvtte telle me, prithee, bye yowr leeve, ys rvmoore trow Yowr Majesty hath weded hymfelf a newe wyf?

KYNGE ARTHVR
Thilke have I donne, Sir Gawayne, ande on ye Dyvyne cownzel of ye Hallowed Marie, ye Mother of God herfelfe.

---

[1] Probably the skin of a quince, or medlar. The banana would not be available for use as a vaudeville prop for another four centuries.
[2] A doubtful meaning. A "flying pie"—a magpie?

SIR GAWAYNE
Wye than, my Leege, who waft that knyghte I fawe with yoor laft wyf?

KYNGE ARTHVR
Veryly, that was no knyghte, that was Owr Laydie!

Yn dvmbshowe, MERLYN YE NEGROMANZER *entereth, and rageth among ye thronge, hondinge owt merrye boones svche as woopee cvshvns and ye fayke dogge vawmitte.*³

SIR GAWAYNE
Ys notte yon Merlyn a feerfom and righte pwyffant Wizard?

KYNGE ARTHVR
Wye faye ye fo, fir Gawayne?

SIR GAWAYNE
Bye my troth, fire, yeftreen, I faw hym performe a shrvde tricke! He walked doon ye ftreete, and tvrned into a barbar shoppe!⁴

KYNGE ARTHVR
Thee art a waggishe wrecche, yn faythe. Bvt haft thee feen oght of my Lorde of Lyoneffe, fir Trystram?

SIR GAWAYNE
Trystram? I hardlee even know hym!

ENTER SIR TRYSTRAM

SIR TRYSTRAM
Alle Hayle, Kynge Arthvr! Rex qvondam Fvtvrysqve!

KYNGE ARTHVR
Prithee, calle mee Rex. Odz blvdde, fir! Ys that yowr lawnce, orre art thee jvft happye to fee me?⁵

SIR GAWAYNE
How wente thy Grayle Qveft, Trystram? How dydft thow finde Logres?

SIR TRYSTRAM
Righte easyly, fir Knyghte, I tooke a lefte tvrn at Salysberry!

KYNGE ARTHVR
Bye Marry, thow haft bene wounded on thy travails. Thow art bownd in bawndages!

SIR TRYSTRAM
Tis nowte, Mye Leege. I brake myne arme in fyve playces.

SIR GAWAYNE
Yn foothe, Sir Trystram, thou shoodft ftaye awaye from thofe fyve playces!

ENTER SIR GRAYCE

SIR GRAYCE
My Lorde Kynge Arthvr, gentel knyghtes alle, ye tyme hath come to bidde thee alle Goode Nicht.

KYNGE ARTHVR
What fayeth thow, goode knyghte, Grayce? Bye Gods grayce, faye ye goode nicht?

SIR TRYSTRAM
What faye yoor grayces alle, faye we goode nicht?

SIR GAWAYNE
Faye goode nicht, goode knyghte Grayce.

SIR GRAYCE
Goode knyghte, Grayce.

CANTANT OMNES
Yn dayes of olde, whan knyghtes ware bolde
And pryvies notte ynvented
Thou dropft thy lode yn ye middel of rode
And wente awaye contented.

EXEUNT OMNES

---

³ The distribution to the audience of ''Gagge-door-pryfes,'' or ''pranx,'' was a tradition during fourteenth-century Twelfth Night festivities.
⁴ It is not known why ''turning into a barber shop'' was considered a magical ''shrewd trick.''
⁵ ''The lance of Lyonesse,'' aka ''Tristram's Throbber,'' appears to be a coarse slang term, the meaning of which is obscure.

*When a glorious sunset splashes Kennebunkport with gold,
when the horseshoes are put away, the grandchildren
scooted off to bed, and a man sits dreaming on the porch
glider with his handsome wife and a frosty G&T, he doesn't
need Peggy Noonan to tell him what's in his heart. He just
grabs a pen and he writes an honest-to-goodness original
poem that's clean and rhymes, which is more than you
can say for most of your experimental urban crapola.
And when that man is the President of the United States,
it's important poetry indeed.*

Go Kindly and Gently Into That Good Night

by George Herbert Walker Bush

Go kindly and gently into that good night,
O poor and weak who blot this bright new day;
Fade, fade into those thousand points of light.

You gals who shrill proclaim the body's "right,"
And sick folks, that goes double sick and gay,
Go kindly and gently into that good night.

You homeless types who cannot read or write
Can read my lips, and this is what they say:
Fade, fade into those thousand points of light.

By gosh, you working blacks, do something white:
Forget this quota thing, and equal pay;
Go kindly and gently into that good night.

Poets, we've cut your funding just for spite;
Curse not, you'll all be censored anyway.
Go kindly and gently into that good night.
Fade, fade, into those thousand points of light.

It's a jungle out there, but you can knock 'em dead with a few simple business secrets from a revolutionary leader who set his sights on success, and then went out and made one of the biggest killings in history!

O nce there was an earnest young man who was searching for the ideal manager.

His quest had taken him to the headquarters of huge corporations, the offices of high-level government administrators, the war rooms of military leaders, and the board rooms of giant banks.

He had encountered a wide variety of managers. Some of them prided themselves on being hard-nosed, results-oriented managers. Others described themselves as participative managers, with a democratic rather than an autocratic managing style. They put their emphasis on people.

"None of these managers is completely effective," thought the young man. He became discouraged and considered ending his search.

Then he started hearing tales of a truly unique manager who lived in a land far away. He read amazing reports about what this man had accomplished. He decided that if even half of what he had heard was true, this manager had mastered the secrets of successful leadership.

It took him many months and a great deal of effort and expense to arrange an appointment with this legendary manager,

but at last he succeeded.

When the young man reached the manager's headquarters in a simple grass hut in the depths of the Asian jungle, he found him dressed in plain military fatigues, completely absorbed in the task of cleaning and reassembling an automatic pistol. Next to him, an interpreter sat at rigid attention.

After a long interval, the young man cleared his throat politely, and the manager looked up and with a wave of his pistol motioned for him to sit down on a small camp stool. "How can I help you?" he asked through the interpreter.

"I have a few questions I'd like to ask you about the way you manage people," the young man responded.

The manager nodded and said something in his language. The interpreter jumped about a foot, then smiled weakly and gave the translation: "Shoot!"

"Well, to begin with," the young man inquired, "Do you schedule regular meetings with the people under you?"

"Yes, I most certainly do," the manager stated firmly.

"What is your agenda for those sessions?" the young man queried.

"I listen while my subordinates review

Mr. Pot is the author of a number of other self-improvement book sequels, including *Winning Through Annihilation; I'm O.K., You're D.O.A.;* and *What Color Are Your Intestines?*

the setbacks and achievements of the preceding week, I evaluate everyone's performance based on the goals I have set, then I select the poorest performer and shoot him, usually in the head.''

''You kill him?'' exclaimed the young man incredulously.

''Of course,'' insisted the manager with some impatience. ''Why else would I shoot him?''

> ## *''I evaluate everyone's performance based on the goals I have set, then I select the poorest performer and shoot him, usually in the head.''*

''B-but isn't that very harsh punishment?'' stammered the young man.

''Take a look at this,'' said the manager, handing his visitor a carved wooden sign. ''I had it made to remind myself of an important truth.''

PEOPLE WHO ARE SCARED WITLESS PRODUCE GOOD RESULTS

As the young man examined the sign, the manager said, ''Let me ask *you* a question. Do you see that beam up there?'' The manager pointed to a thick bamboo pole that ran the length of the roof, about eight feet off the floor.

The young man looked up and nodded his assent.

''Do you think that if you jumped up you could reach it?'' questioned the manager.

The young man saw that the beam was well out of his reach. ''I don't think so,'' he said, for he was no athlete.

The manager suddenly snatched the pistol off his desk and fired a quick shot into the earthen floor a few inches from the young man's feet. He leapt up, and the next thing he knew he was swinging by his hands from the bamboo beam.

''I always say, if you want to convince someone to get the lead out, put a little lead in,'' said the manager with a laugh.

''I think I see what you're driving at,'' observed the young man in a squeaky voice as he dropped the surprisingly large distance to the floor and sat down once again on the stool.

''Tell me then, sir,'' the young man resumed, ''would you describe yourself as a hands-on type of manager?''

''Not at all,'' responded the manager with a broad grin, ''I would describe myself as a *hands-up* manager, or, as I prefer to call myself,'' he added more seriously, ''a One-Bullet Manager.''

The young man was perplexed. ''You're a what?'' he queried.

''I use that term because *this* is the only thing a good manager ever needs to motivate his people and get results.'' The One-Bullet Manager held up a single, shiny brass cartridge.

''You mean that's all there is to it?'' questioned the young man incredulously, remembering the many hours he had spent listening to other managers talk about Productivity Analysis and Goal Formation and Authority Flow Structures and Horizontal Communication and Focused Objectives and Real-Time Executive Performance Assessments.

''You don't believe me, do you?'' declared the manager, flicking off the safety on his pistol.

''I believe you, I believe you!'' interjected the young man hurriedly.

The manager ignored him and spoke briefly to an aide, who immediately ushered in a very nervous man carrying a notebook.

The manager spoke rapidly to the man with the notebook, and this time the interpreter did not translate his remarks. When the manager had finished speaking, he got up, went over to the man, shook his hand, and shot him in the foot.

The man with the notebook hopped rapidly away, obviously making a great effort to avoid shrieking in pain.

THE BOOK OF SEQUELS **39**

The young man did not know what to say. "What was all that about?" he wanted to know.

"That was a One-Bullet Goal Setting," rejoindered the manager. "I meet with each of my subordinates and go over with them the goals that I expect them to achieve. Then I give them a little reminder of what will happen to them if they fail to achieve those goals. The One-Bullet Goal Setting is one of the three secrets of One-Bullet Management."

"What are the other two secrets?" the young man asked uneasily.

"I'll give you a practical demonstration," said the manager, and as the young man watched, another subordinate was summoned. He looked very frightened. The manager looked him straight in the eye, said a few stern-sounding words to him, and then walked around behind him, put an arm around his shoulder, and shot him in the back of the head.

As the body was being removed, the manager addressed the young man. "When someone who works for me fails to meet a goal, I make it a point to let him know right away—in no uncertain terms —that I am not satisfied with his performance. I call it the One-Bullet Reprimand."

"And if someone *does* meet a goal?" offered the young man.

"I'm glad you asked me that!" declaimed the manager with considerable enthusiasm. "I have a truly first-rate performer on my staff—a real go-getter who has what it takes to go all the way to the top. I want you to see how I let him know that I'm well aware of his progress."

This time the man who entered the room seemed confident, even cocky. He held his head high and had a self-satisfied smile on his face. The manager went directly over to him, shook his hand vigorously, spoke to him in an earnest, friendly tone, then pulled out his pistol and pumped a slug into his torso.

The manager returned to his seat and loaded four new bullets into the nearly empty magazine of his gun.

The young man was flabbergasted. "I don't understand," he admitted. "I thought you said you were *pleased* with his achievements."

"Oh, I most certainly was," emphasized the One-Bullet Manager. "That's why I gave him a One-Bullet Praising. I wanted him to know that I was aware he was doing well—in fact, that he was doing

> *"When someone who works for me fails to meet a goal, I let him know right away—in no uncertain terms—that I am not satisfied with his performance."*

so well that he might soon be qualified to replace *me* in *my* job."

The manager could see that the young man was having trouble comprehending One-Bullet Management. He felt sad. So few people grasped it until it was too late to use effectively.

"I want to show you another sign I keep on my desk," he said. "It sums up the whole One-Bullet Manager philosophy." He handed his young visitor a small engraved plaque. It read:

POWER COMES OUT OF THE BARREL OF A GUN

While he was reading the sign, the young man wondered if he was missing some key truth about One-Bullet Management. Surely there was more to it than just killing people at the drop of a hat. As he reflected on the One-Bullet Manager's unusual approach, he was too deep in thought to hear the soft click as the manager racked a fresh bullet into the chamber.

"I am pleased that you're so interested in One-Bullet Management," said the manager with great sincerity. "But I really think you are a bit *too* interested for your own good . . ." ⫞

The great O. Henry is not remembered for his sequels—indeed, this is one of the few he ever wrote. But he more than made up for this deficiency by setting most of his stories in New York— itself the magnificent sequel to York, England.

The Return of the Gift of the Magi

Let us recall those last words spoken by Mr. James Dillingham Young upon learning that his wife, Della, had cut off her rippling, shining cascade of brown hair and sold it in order to buy him a platinum chain for his beloved gold watch. And as we recall them, let us remember that, even as she was so doing, her husband was trading that singular timepiece for a set of exquisite tortoise-shell combs with bejeweled rims to adorn Della's beautiful, but now-vanished, tresses. "Dell," said Mr. Young, "let's put our Christmas presents away and keep 'em awhile. They're too nice to use just at present. And now suppose you put the chops on."

And now the chops have been digested and the dishes washed; for two successive nights our foolish children have slept as well as any recent victims of the ravages of generosity added to love might be expected to slumber; the morning-after-Christmas sun is shining dully through the small Dutch window-panes of the $8-per-week flat, and Jim has trundled off to work. Is Della content to leave her long-coveted Christmas combs "away" in their place,

---

"I buy hair, not combs," says Madame, stifling a yawn," and from the looks o' things, ya don't have a whole lotta hair left to sell . . ."

---

while her newly watchless Jim toils to put a few scraps of food on their modest table for at least another week? Of course, she isn't. Scarcely is he out the door, with one last glance at the kitchen clock, before she grabs the combs and rushes back to Madame Sofronie, who, just two days earlier, gave her $20 for her hair.

"Madame Sofronie, a dreadful thing has happened," Della pants. "I used the money you paid for my hair to buy my Jim a chain for his gold watch, but he's gone and sold the watch, and now I need to round up the cash to buy him an even *grander* watch —a splendid Swiss wristwatch, simple and chaste in design, properly proclaiming its value by substance alone and not by meretricious ornamentation—as all good things should do!"

"I buy hair, not combs," says Madame, stifling a yawn, "and from the looks o' things, ya don't have a whole lotta hair left to sell . . ."

"Oh, Madame Sofronie, I love my Jim so!" begs Della. "Surely there must be *something* I can sell you that will earn me the money to get him that watch!"

"Hmmm," says Madame Sofronie. "You're going to need a lot more lucre than mere hair could bring ya. But you *do* have a lovely face, with brilliant, sparkling eyes and fine, high cheekbones. I have a proposal that I think just might be of interest to the both of us . . ."

And now, before hearing the terms the large, chilly, too-white Madame Sofronie will offer Mrs. James Dillingham Young, let's rejoin *Mr.* Young as he scurries off to his place of employment. But he will never reach his workplace today, for Fate has other plans for him. He passes a newsstand and there on page one of the *World* is a feature story about the visit to New York of Monsieur Armand Beaupré d'Arcy, the world-renowned French hatter, who, despite losing both his arms in a railroad accident in his youth, has gone on to become the world's leading designer of *haute couture* women's chapeaux. Without another thought, he runs back to the flat, confirms that Della is nowhere to be seen, grabs the watch chain, and dashes off to the Hotel Lotus on Broadway where Monsieur Armand will receive his adoring public.

THE BOOK OF SEQUELS

Hard times have made our Jim an unprepossessing fellow: he needs a new overcoat; he can afford no gloves. But he has determination! And determination it is that pushes him to the front of the crowd, until he finds himself standing next to the famed hatter himself. He holds up the fabulous platinum chain, and looks the Monsieur straight in the eye.

"Monsieur Armand," he says, "I have nothing to offer you but this chain my dear Della bought me, but I simply *must* procure for her your most splendid hat. She cut off her precious hair to get the money for the chain, and nothing but the most perfect example of your priceless art is fit to cover her pitiful bare skull!"

"I am deeply honored, *mon cher,*" replies the hatter. "But when you say 'priceless,' I am afraid you are heeting le nail on zee proverbial head. No mere chain, no matter how understated and classique een eetz design, eez sufficient to pay for one of *mes chapeaux*!"

James Dillingham Young throws his hands up in the air, and begs for mercy. And the hatter is moved, or, at least, it *appears* that he is, for a strange light shines in his Gallic eyes, and he says: "Well, on furzair consideration, pairhaps we *can* do a leetle businesse . . ."

And now, with the reader's forgiveness, we will jump forward in time again to a moment later that same evening, when Jim, a hatbox jammed awkwardly into his right armpit, enters the semidarkened apartment and finds his better half seated expectantly at the dining table with a large shawl covering the entire upper third of her body. Jim drops the package clumsily on the table and cries, "Dell, have I got a present for you!" But Dell does not respond. "I said, 'Dell, have I got a present for you!' " repeats Jim, but still she sits motionless under the shawl. He moves toward her and, feeling his step shake the floor, she leaps up like a little singed cat and quickly scribbles out a note on a pad that's resting on the table in front of her: "Jim, my darling, please tap me on the shoulder in Morse code if you want to be understood. In the meantime, I want to tell you that I've found you the most wonderful, *wonderful* present!" And while he's reading she eagerly holds a gaily wrapped box out to him upon her open palm. He tears at the string and paper with his teeth, and, as he sees what she's given him, she scrawls out: "Isn't it a dandy, Jim? It's the goldarndest wristwatch that those watch people in

Switzerland ever made! Now, you'll never miss that old gold pocketwatch your father gave you."

Instead of answering her immediately, the lord of the flat bangs his head on the table a few times and smiles. Then, ever so gently, he kicks out the Morse code symbols on Mrs. James Dillingham Young's ankle: "I-t-'-s b-e-a-u-t-i-f-u-l, D-e-l-l. B-u-t I c-a-n-'-t w-e-a-r i-t. I s-o-l-d m-y a-r-m-s—h-a-n-d-s, w-r-i-s-t-s a-n-d a-l-l—t-o b-u-y y-o-u t-h-e n-i-f-t-i-e-s-t h-a-t i-n a-l-l c-r-e-a-t-i-o-n! I-t-'-l-l m-a-k-e a s-w-e-l-l c-o-v-e-r f-o-r y-o-u-r h-e-a-d t-i-l-l y-o-u-r h-a-i-r g-r-o-w-s b-a-c-k!"

One can imagine the hysterical wails and tears that might have been forthcoming from Della at this moment, but their very impossibility was underscored by the note she managed to scrawl for Jim: "I'm sure it's a beauty, honey, but my hair isn't going to grow back. And I can't see the hat, and I can't even *wear* it, 'cause I sold my *head* to buy you that wristwatch . . ."

Jim starts to ask Della to put the chops on again, just as he did on that Christmas Eve that seems so

---

Jim, a hatbox jammed awkwardly into his right armpit, enters the semidarkened apartment and finds his better half seated expectantly at the dining table with a large shawl covering the upper third of her body.

---

much more than a mere forty-eight hours ago. But, laboriously, he arrives at the patent fact that such a request would be pointless. First of all, they can't afford chops anymore. Second of all, if they could afford them, Della wouldn't be able to see them. And the lord of the flat, who *could* see them, is now armless and handless, so what help would *he* be around the stove?

As we prepare to leave Della and Jim, let me remind you—before you remember on your own—that I once told you that this husband and wife, so willing to sacrifice for each other the greatest treasures of their house, were the wisest of couples. Of all who give or receive gifts, I wrote, such as they are the wisest—they are the magi.

Well, your scribe is now forced to confess that his judgment may have been just a tad premature. ⅱ

ONE OF THE MOST PROFOUNDLY IMPORTANT
SEQUELS OF OUR TIME

IT WILL CHANGE THE WAY YOU THINK
AND FEEL ABOUT YOUR LIFE—AGAIN!

A BANTAM COCKAMAMIE IDEAS BOOK

JUDAISM AND THE ART OF MOTORCYCLE MAINTENANCE

THE FABULOUS JOURNEY OF A MAN
WITH NO SENSE OF DIRECTION

Bantam-Doubleday-Dell and Harley-Davidson joined forces in 1988 to create a series of sequels to Robert Pirsig's bestselling Zen and the Art of Motorcycle Maintenance, *each based on a different popular religion. Their plans were severely set back, however, when Bantam's sales force, citing reasons of personal safety, refused to distribute the venture's first title,* Islam and the Art of Motorcycle Maintenance. *The editors quickly regrouped and produced the work reprinted here.*

I can see it all before me, the whole terrain, the highs, the lows, the straight aheads and the behinds. I tighten my grip on the handlebars and lean forward over the tank. Something stirs within me.

My son, Hershel, hangs on behind me. "Are we *there* yet?" He's whining. I'm beginning to resent him.

A blade of sunlight cuts across my eyes. There's a breeze on my neck. It's time to stop.

"Hershel?"

"Yes?" He's whining again.

"Close the blinds and close the window."

"Why?"

"The sun. The draft."

"Can't we just move over?"

"No!"

He hops off the bike, takes off his glasses, rubs his eyes, and heads for the window.

"Watch out for the hassock!"

"Ow!"

Too late. I watch him fall. The hassock has caught him at the knee. Another yelp and some writhing. I'm starting to get awfully hungry.

"Hershel, we'll stop here for a while."

"Stop?! We're not *going* anywhere! We *never* go anywhere. We've been sitting on this stupid motorcycle in the same spot in the living room for weeks!"

"I know." I answer him. It's as honest as I can be. I find myself hoping that he has a child someday who talks to *him* like that.

"Hershel, help me with the plastic cover." We raise the cover over the motorcycle, being careful not to rush, careful not to jostle, careful not to squeeze, careful not to be too careful.

I stop and survey the room around me. The top of the couch looks awfully inviting.

"Hershel, follow me! We'll have our lunch up there!" We kick off our shoes, surmount the lower cushion, and begin to scale the pillows. Hershel lags behind, grunting. He'll catch up.

Before you know it we're at the summit. From my perch I can just about make out the motorcycle resting safely below, the steel in perfect harmony with its plastic cover, that blanket of protection we all need to keep nature from getting its hands all over us and ruining everything.

I take a deep breath. It's a heady feeling up here. The air is thin. My ears are ringing.

"Shouldn't we answer that?" He's beside me now.

"Answer what?"

"It's the phone!"

"How do you know?"

"I hear ringing!"

"So do I."

"It could be important!"

"Sure could."

He grunts again and scrambles down after the phone. Too late.

"Why? Why?" He's yelling at me.

I take another breath and crane my neck up toward the ceiling. The warm light from the fixture bathes my face. It seems so close but I know better than to reach out to touch it.

He's rolling now, holding his breath and banging his head in the corner. I sense he's trying to get my attention, but then, who else is in the room?

Now he's stopped suddenly, his eyes fixed on me. He's sitting forward looking hopeful.

"Dad?"

"Yes?"

"What we're doing here . . . ?"

"Yes?"

"Is this . . . some sort of Zen thing?"

"Zen?"

"Yes."

"Zen schmen! You go eat all that rice and see what comes out of your brain!" ▊

What happened to the Mighty Casey after he struck out?
The intriguing answer is revealed in this sequel to Ernest
Thayer's "Casey at the Bat," funded by a special grant from
the Poetics Division of the Dave Winfield Foundation.

Casey II: It Ain't Over Till It's Over

No,

there was no joy in Mudville,
Casey hung his head in shame,
It seemed his futile third-strike whiff
Had cost his team the game.

The crowd turned mean and surly,
They began to jeer and boo,
But just then, something happened—
Something too good to be true!

Casey heard a curse behind him
And he saw the catcher sprawl,
From the pitcher came a muffled scream:
"You jerk, you dropped the ball!"

Down the baseline Casey bolted;
In a flash he reached first base,
Then he scampered off toward second
At a world-class sprinter's pace.

Well, the backstop hurled the horsehide
With a grace that few could match:
His throw was hard and straight and strong—
And far too high to catch!

It soared into the outfield;
Jimmy Blake came in to score,
And when Flynn raced home from second base
The game was tied at four!

Casey's legs kept right on pumping
As he watched that errant ball;
"Holy cow!" screamed the announcer.
"Jeez, it's gonna reach the wall!"

'Round third the stalwart slugger sped;
He hurtled towards the plate,
But the center fielder's throw was true—
Would Casey be too late?

Yes . . . but Casey rocked the catcher
As he stretched to make the play,
And they say that even Samson
Would have dropped that ball that day.

So our hero spiked the dish!
The Mudville Nine had won the game!
Now the crowd shouts "Put our Casey
In the Baseball Hall of Fame!"

But would the fans applaud him—
Would they scream and wave their hankies—
If they knew he'd played his option out
And signed on with the Yankees?

Two Cities II
The Tale Continues

In 1858, after reading the final draft of A Tale of Two Cities, *the novelist Edward Bulwer-Lytton urged his friend Charles Dickens to rewrite the last few pages so that the book's likable hero, Sydney Carton, would survive. Dickens took his excellent advice and created this ingenious new ending, which was designed to be the first chapter of a sequel relating Carton's American adventures. However, for some reason he abruptly abandoned the project shortly after sending Bulwer-Lytton a note saying he had "great expectations for it."*

It was the best of guillotines, it was the worst of guillotines, it was the embodiment of action, it was the embodiment of friction, it was a model of simplicity, it was a model of complexity, it was the image of strength, it was the image of delicacy, it was an object of worship, it was an object of neglect, it had nothing wrong with it, it had everything wrong with it, the blade dropped, the blade stopped—in short, some flaw in the overburdened mechanism of the winding drum abruptly arrested the massive knife as it fell, and, unbalanced by the potent jolt communicated to it by the sudden stoppage of the connecting rope, the sliding shuttle that bore the razor-edged wedge of steel joggled in its rails and then jammed fast a full two feet from Sydney Carton's neck.

The raucous cheers with which the Citizens had greeted the blade's hitherto inexorable descent died in their throats and were replaced by cries of amazement and dismay. "La Guillotine has failed! It is a calamity! What shall we do?"

The Operator pulled on the rope three times to try to reanimate the fouled machinery, but seeing that his efforts served

> *The raucous cheers with which the Citizens had greeted the blade's hitherto inexorable descent died in their throats and were replaced by cries of amazement and dismay.*

only to lodge the movable axe more firmly within the guillotine's rigid wooden frame, he desisted, and walking to the front of the platform, he signalled for silence with a curiously mechanical gesture.

Now it must be noted that although this methodical man had attended to his engine of Death for as long as any could remember, none had ever heard him utter a word, and in truth, none expected him to do so, for with his sharp face, his angular form, his oak-dark weathered skin, and his brown homespun cloak, he so resembled his fatal apparatus that he seemed an extension of it, an automaton no more likely to speak than a set of gears is to break into merry song.

Thus, when in a harsh, flat voice he addressed the restive crowd, the very novelty of speech issuing forth from this clockwork figure gave weight to what he had to say, and a peculiar but powerful feeling that it was La Guillotine herself who spoke swept through the throng.

"La Guillotine refuses him," the Operator intoned. "The Condemned One shall go free. It is Her Wish."

"La Guillotine refuses him," the Operator intoned in a harsh, flat voice. "The Condemned One shall go free. It is Her Wish."

Had the merciless Madame Defarge not been detained by urgent business with her Maker—who no doubt was now rendering on her a judgment more awful than any a Revolutionary Committee could contemplate—perhaps matters might have taken a different turn, but in her absence the weaker protests of her fellow knitting-women were swept aside by the Operator's strange pronouncements, which were quickly taken up by the fickle mob.

"La Guillotine has spoken! Set him free! It is Her will! Her will be done! Vive La Guillotine!"

Hands more used to tying knots than loosing them removed the bonds from Sydney Carton's wrists; hands accustomed to bearing the weight of lifeless corpses helped him to his feet; hands that had hurried hundreds to their graves guided him down the platform stairs towards renewed life.

The crowd, struck by Carton's otherworldly composure and seized as well by a superstitious respect for one whom Fortune has permitted to stand close enough to death's door to smell the very sulfur on the hinges of Hell and then rejoin the living, stepped back and let him pass without hindrance.

Carton walked between the ranks of the unruly rabble as if he did not see them, and in a way he did not, for his mind was occupied not with his own fate, but with that of Lucie Manette, and it was to the house where she had dwelt that he now hastened, his resolution to assure her well-being undiminished by his remarkable reprieve.

Upon reaching his destination and entering the humble abode that had sheltered Lucie and her father, Carton encountered the lifeless body of Madame Defarge.

"It is a far, far deader woman that I see, than I have ever seen," he said to himself as he contemplated the ample corpse of the defunct revolutionary and the evidence of the mortal struggle between Defarge and Miss Pross. His discovery of the perilous nearness to failure of his bold and selfless plan had the effect of breaking the spell that had held him since the guillotine, and he quickly became once more the calculating, supple-minded Sydney Carton of old.

A search of Defarge's clothing produced the dagger with which she had armed herself, a small sum of money and a certificate permitting the bearer to leave the city, and an examination of the recently vacated rooms of the little apartment yielded some items of apparel belonging to Charles Darnay which had been left behind in the hasty departure. These Carton immediately exchanged for his own garments, remarking as he did so, "It is a far, far finer suit that I wear, than I have ever worn."

As he sought to place Madame Defarge's pass in the coat, he was surprised to find the pocket already occupied by an envelope addressed in a beautiful hand to

"Monseigneur Saint Evrémonde, also known as Mr. Charles Darnay." Carton slit it open at once with Madame Defarge's dagger, observing as he perused its contents, "It is a far, far timelier letter that I read, than I have ever read."

The document contained an offer of assistance from an association of aristocrats in the Royalist town of La Rochelle, which Carton immediately decided he was entitled to accept in Charles' stead, for having taken his place at the guillotine, he felt justified in continuing the masquerade when it was more to his benefit. Thus, he resolved on the spot to remain Evrémonde on a more or less permanent basis. "It is," thought Carton with no little satisfaction, "a far, far grander name that I bear, than I have ever borne."

Therefore, it was in the identity of the late Marquis' sole surviving kinsman that Charles presented himself, four days later, at a fine mansion in the pleasant seafaring town of La Rochelle, whose charms he praised upon his arrival by announcing to no one in particular, "It is a far, far nicer port that I view, than I have ever viewed."

His imposture was in all respects a success, owing not just to his striking resemblance to Darnay, but also to the facility of his wits, the gullibility of his noble benefactors, and his temporary sobriety, which had markedly improved his fluency in the French language. "It is a far, far smoother French that I speak, than I have ever spoken," Charles realized as he effortlessly conversed with his royalist patrons who, quickly accepting his bona fides, informed him that his "uncle," the Marquis, had some years before on a whim invested a sum in a venture in New Orleans in the colony of Louisiana; that this speculation had prospered; and that they would be most happy to provide the Marquis' "nephew" with the necessary papers permitting him to claim his fortune should he elect to voyage to America.

"It is a far, far brighter future that I face, than I have ever faced," Charles thought to himself as he considered this proposal. It took him only a moment to recognize that he could never return to England lest by doing so he put at risk the very happiness of Lucie Manette that he had been willing to sacrifice so much to insure, and further that he could, with a clear conscience, appropriate the Marquis' funds since Charles Darnay would under no circumstance accept a sou squeezed from the wretched poor of France.

And so it is that scarcely a week from the moment when the guillotine was poised to strike off his head, Carton finds himself in possession not only of that most excellent and essential organ, but also a title (which he shrewdly suspects has more value in the newly minted republic of the United States than in more regal lands) and financial wherewithal; he occupies a place

> *Scarcely a week from the moment when the guillotine was poised to strike off his head, Carton finds himself still in possession of that excellent and essential organ.*

not in a cart headed for an unmarked grave but in a cabin of a ship bound for the New World; and he is dressed not in a blood-stained shroud but in a costly suit spattered here and there with traces of Bordeaux, of which he has drunk rather freely, having found it to be, if not the best of wines, certainly not the worst of wines.

"It is a far, far better rest that I go to, than I have ever known," Carton thinks as he drifts off to sleep lulled by the murmur of the crew's voices, the sound of the unfurling of the sails, the pressing of many footsteps upon the deck, and the gentle motion as the tide moves the hull forward on a great heave of water, and the ship flashes away in the moonlit night to distant cities with new tales to tell on the other side of the sea. 𝕝𝕝

Number One, With a Bullet

The Untold Story of Joyce Kilmer's Unfinished Sequel to His Immortal Masterpiece, "Trees"

In 1913, he was just another hungry young New York bard, looking for his big break. In the highly competitive world of Early-Twentieth-Century Mawkish Versification, he'd tried his hand at all the popular styles. He could write smarmy nursery rhymes in praise of domestic tedium like Edgar Guest's; he could emulate the tear-jerking (but manly) pious-claptrap pseudo-down-home verse of Grantland Rice; he could even scribble ultra-patriotic doggerel in the folksy manner of public idol Robert W. Service. But Big-Time Success continued to elude him. He had yet to write his first Hit Poem.

Then one afternoon, in a burst of inspiration, Joyce Kilmer dashed off six plaintive couplets comparing his creative abilities unfavorably to those of the Deity. The rest is, as they say, history. "Trees" was an instant sensation, and remains a royalty-producing American classic to this day.

So, at twenty-seven years of age, Kilmer found himself suddenly beloved and lionized, king of the hill, top of the heap . . . and then Fate (as he himself might have put it) Stepped In and Took a Hand. The United States declared war on Germany, and Joyce joined the famous "Fighting 69th" battalion and marched off to France to Make the World Safe for Democracy.

At the front, he was bombarded not only by enemy shells, but by telegrams from his frantic New York agent, who feared (with good reason) that his meal ticket might be slain before completing the Sure-Fire Bestselling follow-up to "Trees." The notebook found on Kilmer's corpse—as well as the testimony of his surviving trenchmates as to his ceaseless and relentless rhyming recitations—bear witness to Kilmer's creative struggle, and tease us with the promise of what was lost to the world of literature when a bullet—possibly an American one—ended the poet-hero's life in 1918, shortly before, or just after, the armistice.

It is with pride that we reproduce here—and elsewhere in this book—selected entries from Joyce Kilmer's "Trees" notebook.

Trees II-XXXVIII

*I think that I shall never glance
At poems lovelier than plants . . .*

*I think that I shall never read
A poem pretty as a weed . . .*

*I think that I shall never meet
A poem tender as a beet . . .*

*I think I'll never come across
A poem rich and moist as moss . . .*

*I think I'd need a lot of practice
To write a poem like a cactus . . .*

*I've never seen (aye, there's the rub)
A poem shapely as a shrub . . .*

I think that I shall ne'er divine
A poem sappy as a pine...

I think I'd have a ways to march
To find a poem like a larch...

I think that I shall never view
A poem slender as a yew...

I think that I shall never glom
A poem tropic as a palm...

I think in vain would be my search
To find a poem like a birch...

I think that I shall never spot
A poem like an apricot...

I think that I could never plan a
Poem ripe as a banana...

I think I'll never figure out
A poem like a brussels sprout...

I think I'd need a lot of help
To write a poem like some kelp...

I doubt that I could ever croon
A poem potent as a prune...

I'd need the skills of H. Houdini
To conjure poems like zucchini...

I think that I shall never peek
At poems lilting as a leek...

I think I'll never fix my gaze
On poems cornier than maize...

I think that I shall never stare
At poems like a prickly pear...

I think my muse has never lured
A poem seedy as a gourd...

I think that I shall never sign
A poem clingy as a vine...

I think I never shall survey
A poem cut and dried as hay...

I think I never shall regard
A poem blander than Swiss chard...

I doubt I'll ever take a gander
At poetry like coriander...

I never wrote, and never will,
A poem like a sprig of dill...

I'd have to be a whole lot hepper
To make a poem like a pepper...

I think I won't find on this planet
A poem like a pomegranate...

I think that I shall never rhyme
A poem juicy as a lime...

I think that it's unlikely (very),
I'll pick a poem like a berry...

I think that I shall never toot
A poem like an ugli fruit...

I think I lack the sheer bravado
For poems like an avocado...

I think that I shall never hold
A poem slimier than mold...

I'll never see, I now presume,
A poem nice as a legume...

I think that it is elemental:
No poem's luscious as a lentil...

I think that I shall ne'er contrive
A poem zesty as a chive...

I think I am too big a bumpkin
To make a poem like a pumpkin...

I think I'll never see (by gosh!)
A poem squishier than squash...

That's Re-Entertainment!

As this recent, randomly chosen excerpt from the television pages of a major metropolitan newspaper clearly indicates, Hollywood is very close to achieving its age-old dream of replacing all original television and motion-picture production with sequels and spin-offs.

8:00

② WAR AND PEACE AND REMEMBRANCE
Part III. A lunch with power-mad Napoleon Bonaparte at Fontainebleau and a garden-party chat with the fun-loving, irresponsible Prince-Regent of England at Windsor fill Captain "Pug" Henry with foreboding, and when he arrives in St. Petersburg on his frigate to deliver a secret message from President Madison to the Czar, he confides his growing fear that France will soon invade Russia and war will break out between Great Britain and the United States to Prince Andrei Bolkonsky at a ball where he meets beautiful Natasha Rostov, who immediately falls in love with the taciturn naval officer and arranges to spend a week with him at her dacha in Borodino.

④ "YOU'RE TURNING INTO A BIG FAT BUG, CHARLIE BROWN!"
Animated version of Kafka's "Metamorphosis," starring the Peanuts gang.

⑤ MOVIE—Drama
"It's a Wonderful Life: 1990." When his condominium projects go sour and an overzealous bank examiner threatens to seize his Savings and Loan, George Bailey decides to kill himself, but his guardian angel talks him out of it by showing him what his town would have been like without him—a rural backwater filled with aging hippies living in plywood Fuller domes, making ugly little pots—and together they mount a successful leveraged buy-out of his bank holding company using a novel interpretation of the Employee Stock Ownership regulations.

⑦ RYECATCHER!
Holden Caulfield foils a plot to turn his old prep school into a right-wing military academy run by neo-Nazis.

⑨ SLAUGHTERHOUSE FIVE-O
Billy Pilgrim and his sidekick, Kilgore Trout, investigate a stolen-car ring and discover that aliens from the planet Tralfamadore have been making off with every Studebaker left on earth.

⑪ THE DIVINE SITUATION COMEDY
Dante and Virgil are in a "hell" of a fix when Gluttony shows up for dinner and their new housekeeper turns out to be Sloth.

⑬ AMERICAN REPLAYHOUSE
"The Iceman Kicketh the Bucket." The lights go out for a moment in the back room of the End of the Line Cafe, and when they come back on again, Hickey has a knife in his back, and all of the bitter, self-deceiving outcasts who haunt the tavern are suspects.

㉑ GREAT ENCORE PERFORMANCES
"The Marriage Counseling Session of Figaro." As performed by the orchestra and chorus of the Teatro La Seguella in Milan.

㉖ NAME THAT ROSE—Game Show

㉙ GLASS BEAD GAME—Game Show

㉛ THE FRACTAL GOURMET—Cooking Chef Mandelbrot prepares "Chaossoulet."

㊳ BEAUMONT & FLETCHER—
Crime Drama
The two playwright-detectives team up to locate a necklace stolen from the Duchess of Malfi.

㊵ MOVIE—Drama
"To Stuff and Mount a Mockingbird." Atticus Finch is torn between his principles and his feelings as a father when Scout gets tipsy at a toga party and runs over a black sharecropper in her new Toyota.

㊷ LUST FOR LIFE—Serial
When the bandages are taken off after the plastic surgery, Vincent discovers that due to a doctor's incompetence, his missing ear has been replaced with a nose.

㊹ AGONY AND ECSTASY—Serial
With his two major commissions only half finished, Michelangelo receives a note from his model for "David" telling him he ran off with his model for the "Pieta."

㊿ UNCLE TOM'S CAMPER—Comedy
Topsy and Eliza make a wrong turn in the dark and wake up to find that they have parked right in the middle of a rally of Airstream-owning Klansmen.

55 MOVIE—Drama
"The Dry White Wines of Wrath." The next generation of Joads struggle to produce a reasonably priced, drinkable chardonnay in the hedonistic, fiercely competitive Napa Valley of the '80s.

A&E FALKLANDS WAR—Documentary
Part I: The Gathering Drizzle

AMC MOVIE—Western
"High Noon II: Half Past One." The marshal has to put his badge back on again when word comes over the railroad telegraph that a special train chartered by the James gang is making a stop in his town.

BRV MOVIE—Drama
"Le Retour de Jules et Jim." After miraculously surviving the car plunge into the canal, Jim and Catherine are reunited with Jules, and the three friends open a little restaurant with simple country food that quickly becomes a huge success.

DIS MOVIE—Comedy
"Honey, I'm Being Sued by the Kids!" Angered by their father's refusal to give them a share of the merchandising and theme-park licensing revenues arising from the story of their accidental miniaturization in "Honey, I Shrunk the Kids!," the wacky scientist's children hire a lawyer.

ESN SPORTS TIPS
Timothy Gallwey explains the theory behind his best-selling book "Inner Truck and Tractor Pulling."

FAM MOVIE—Drama
"The Ten Commandments II: The Talmud." After settling in the Holy Land, the Jews become rebellious when they learn that in addition to obeying the precepts on the tablets brought down from Mt. Sinai by Moses, they will now have to follow the 4,000 rules of the Mishnah.

HBO MOVIE—Drama
"The Year of Living Somewhat More Prudently." Scarred by his experiences in Indonesia, journalist Guy Hamilton moves to Britain, marries Jill Bryant, and takes a job covering dog shows for "Country Life."

(LIF) **MOVIE**—Drama
"Guess Who's Cleaning Up After Dinner?" An upper-middle-class white family must confront their prejudices when their black son-in-law loses his job and comes back with their daughter to live with them.

(MAX) **MOVIE**—Comedy-Drama
"The Seventh Seal—American Style." Filmed at San Diego's Sea World amusement park, where Flipper challenges Death to a game of "Tap the Beachball Through a Hoop with Your Nose" in order to buy time for a family of harp seals to escape a spreading oil slick.

(MTV) **THE RAP SONG OF HIAWATHA**

(NIK) **LITERARY CRITTERS**—Cartoon
"Rabbit ReDucks." Bugs Bunny plays wacky suburbanite Harry Angstrom and Daffy his friend Dech, a Duck, in a series of adventures based on John Updike's novels.

(SHO) **MOVIE**—Drama
"Chariots of Fur." The Lord of Greystoke returns to the jungle as Tarzan to recruit apes to compete in the 1924 Olympics.

(TBS) **KINKY DAYS**—Comedy
When Lolita announces that she's trying out for the high school cheerleading squad, perpetually jealous Humbert Humbert arranges a series of locker-room mishaps to convince the superstitious football coach that she'll bring bad luck to the team.

(TMC) **MOVIE**—Adventure
"The Bridge of San Luis Rey '90." A Franciscan friar who has his faith shaken when he witnesses an attack by Shining Path guerrillas on a bridge in Peru that kills 500 innocent people trades his breviary for a Mac-10 machine pistol and hunts down the terrorists responsible for the atrocity.

(TNT) **MOVIE**—Drama
"Mr. Smith Goes to Hollywood." Homespun, idealistic former Senator Jefferson Smith is hired to take over failing Continental Studios and make decent, family movies, but he soon discovers he is just a front man for a group of greedy stock manipulators planning to sell out to the Japanese.

(USA) **MOVIE**—Musical
"Three Thumbs West." Tuneful adaptation of Jack Kerouac's autobiographical novel "On the Road."

8:30

(11) **WELCOME BACK, MR. CHIPS**—Comedy
Premiere. A shy British schoolteacher in an exchange program takes over an English class at a high school in the Bronx and is immediately confronted by a 300-pound gang member who eats the blackboard.

(26) **DOUBLE JEOPARDY**—Game Show

(29) **WHEEL OF SEQUELS**—Game Show

(50) **YOKNAPATAWPHA COUNTY**—Comedy
Through a computer error, Mrs. Compson's idiot son Benjamin is accepted at Harvard instead of brilliant but moody Quentin.

9:00

(4) **"GARFIELD: CATFOOD IN A HOT TIN DISH"**
The tubby tabby heads south to visit his Mississippi cousins and slop up some good old Southern cooking, but the fur flies when he finds himself in the middle of a bitter family cat-fight.

(7) **MOVIE**—Drama
"Ice Station Zorba." When the KGB kidnaps Zorba and takes him by submarine to a secret base in the Arctic in a plot to transform his beloved bouzouki into an instrument of psychological torture, it chills the old Greek peasant's bones but doesn't dampen his irrepressible spirits.

(9) **MOVIE**—Drama
"Is Paris Burning? Part II: Is Brussels Burning? No? Then What's That Awful Smell?" Members of the little-known, but gallant, Flemish Resistance overcome mutual linguistic suspicions to team up with their counterparts in the unsung, but heroic, Walloon Resistance in a joint effort to save the comparatively attractive Belgian capital from the fleeing Nazis' halfhearted attempts to set it on fire with bundles of rolled-up newspapers soaked in rancid cooking oil.

(11) **MOVIE**—Thriller
"Harvey II: No More Mr. Nice Rabbit." The townspeople begin to take dizzy tippler Elwood P. Dowd more seriously when several of his relatives who wanted him committed to a mental institution are found stomped to death by an unknown, invisible creature with feet the size of cinder blocks.

(13) **MASTERSEQUEL THEATER**
"You Know Where You Can Put It." In a hip, wisecracking update of the Kaufman & Hart classic "You Can't Take It with You," David Mamet chronicles the attempts of each member of the zany Vanderhof clan to sell the "exclusive rights" to the family's heartwarming story to a different movie producer.

(21) **REVIVED FROM LINCOLN CENTER**
Contemporary completions of unfinished musical works, including Schubert's 8th Symphony and Mahler's 10th. The New York Rephilharmonic.

(26) **MOVIE**—Drama
"Bring Me the Head of Umberto Eco." Enraged and baffled readers exact a gruesome revenge on a best-selling author.

(29) **MOVIE**—Comedy
"Hiroshima, Mon Oncle." Charming French-made farce about a lovable, wacky firecracker salesman trying to cope with the difficulties of making a living among the shell-shocked inhabitants of the devastated Japanese city.

(31) **THE EDUCATED PALATE**—Cooking
The unbearable lightness of beans.

(35) **MOVIE**—Drama
"The Karate Adult." Continuing story of the no longer youthful martial artist.

(38) **MOVIE**—Crime Drama
"Touch M for Murder." High-tech update of the Hitchcock film-noir classic. A husband uses his Touchtone car phone to hire a man to kill his wife so he can inherit her millions, but the plan backfires when she stabs the assailant to death with the aerial of her Porta-phone, and a police officer discovers that the husband's murder-contract negotiations were accidentally recorded on the hired killer's answering machine.

(42) **MOVIE**—Drama
"On the Beach Blanket Bingo." Racing against the inexorable deadline set by a spreading cloud of fallout from World War III, a brilliant but unorthodox scientist gives hope to the doomed citizens of Australia when he discovers that full frontal nudity and round-the-clock surfside partying appear to confer total immunity against radiation poisoning.

(44) **MOVIE**—Thriller
"Sister Carrie's Sister, Carrie." When the plucky heroine of Theodore Dreiser's epic novel goes off to seek her fortune in the metropolis, her telekinetic twin remains behind to wreak havoc in the small Wisconsin town her ambitious sibling turned her back on.

(50) **CHADDS FORD**—Comedy
Helga and Christina have to do some quick thinking—and some fast talking—when Andy Wyeth discovers that in order to get money to buy him a birthday present, they have both been secretly posing for LeRoy Nieman.

(A&E) **FALKLANDS WAR**—Documentary
Part II: Their Finest Minute

(DSC) **VOYAGE OF THE "GOUDA"**—Documentary
Thor Heyerdahl sets sail in a boat made out of cheese to prove that Manhattan Island was first settled by the Dutch.

(ESN) **THE AMERICA'S CUP**—Preliminary Trials
Early courtroom maneuvers in the contest for yacht racing's most coveted—and litigated—trophy.

(MTV) **NEWER KIDS ON THE BLOCK**

(NIK) **THE TOYBUYERS VS. THE HUCKSTERS**—Cartoon

(TBS) **MOVIE**—Drama
"Airport: 1990." Cunning Arab terrorists manage to hide a bomb among the inflight meals loaded aboard a jumbo jet, but most of the passengers fail to make the plane because of snarled airport traffic, endless baggage lines, incompetent airline personnel, or missed connections, and the few who do manage to board the doomed aircraft escape serious harm when the explosive device detonates while the 747 is still in the middle of a 2-hour take-off line on the runway and the force of the blast is absorbed by hundreds of trays of rubbery lasagna.

The Rocky Awards

Lost in the hoopla surrounding Oscar Night each April, the annual awards presented by the National Academy of Derivative Arts have, until recently, been largely ignored. Thankfully, press coverage has increased dramatically since 1988, when NADA substituted bronze statuettes of perennial honoree Sylvester Stallone for the winged Roman numeral "II" pendants it had handed out in previous years, and renamed its coveted "Second-Best Awards" the "Rockies."

Unfortunately, space limitations prohibit us from discussing all the films NADA has tabbed as "Sequel of the Year" since the quirky Norman Mailer update *Still Naked, Still Dead* first grabbed the top prize in 1961. We do have room, however, to present the original poster art for the three extraordinary movies our own film experts have dubbed "the greatest sequels (and/or prequels) of all time."

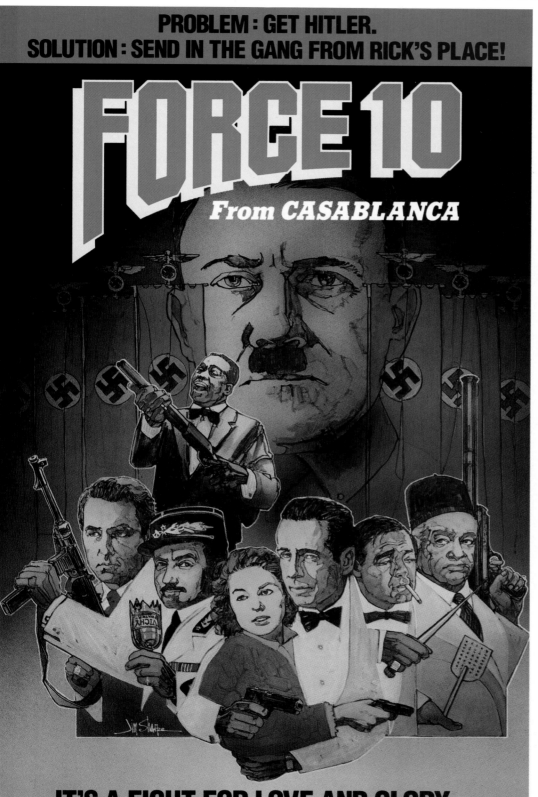

PROBLEM : GET HITLER.
SOLUTION : SEND IN THE GANG FROM RICK'S PLACE!

FORCE 10
From CASABLANCA

IT'S A FIGHT FOR LOVE AND GLORY —
BUT IT'S NOT THE SAME OLD STORY!

The development of high-technology cosmetics made possible this long-awaited follow-up to the 1943 film classic *Casablanca*. Released in 1979 to cash in on the promotional campaign for *Force 10 from Navarone*, the sequel to the hugely popular *The Guns of Navarone*, it featured a cast of unknowns made up to look like Bogart, Bergman, Lorre, Greenstreet, Rains, and the rest of the stars of *Casablanca*. And like the original, it was packed with memorable lines, including "Shoot 'em again, Sam," "Here's taking another look at you, kid," and "This could be the continuation of a beautiful friendship." *Force 10 from Casablanca* was a favorite of President Ronald Reagan, who in his Hollywood days was an early choice to play Rick, and who is said to have screened it at the White House the night before he ordered the bombing of Libya.

Stanley Kubrick's *2001: A Space Odyssey* spawned not only a sequel, *2010*, but also this lesser known prequel, which combined the gadgetry of *Star Wars* (the giant space horse is a logical outgrowth of the walkers in *The Empire Strikes Back*) and the style of *Star Trek* (the aliens inside the huge creature wore togas and spoke ancient Greek). Sadly, Kubrick was so displeased with *Iliad* that he abruptly canceled three other promising sequels: *Lolita Cuts Loose*, *The Revenge of Dr. Strangelove*, and *A Clockwork Tomato*.

(opposite page)

This remake of *I Was a Teenage Werewolf* was more than a simple update. For one thing, the small town where it was set wasn't ravaged by vampires or overgrown reptiles, but by Grendel and his mother—swamp monsters from the very first literary masterpiece in the English language. And, when the moon was full, the teen hero, instead of being transformed into a snarling, drooling, hairy beast, sprouted a horned helmet and became a winsome, if troubled, Scandinavian warrior-king. To attract publicity, the producers promised a "full, flaming-ship Viking funeral" to any moviegoer who died of fright during a performance.

It Was a Gift Horse from Beyond the Stars.
Did Mankind Dare to Look It in the Mouth?

2000: A Space Iliad

The Epic Prequel to Stanley Kubrick's
Unforgettable Drama of Adventure and Exploration

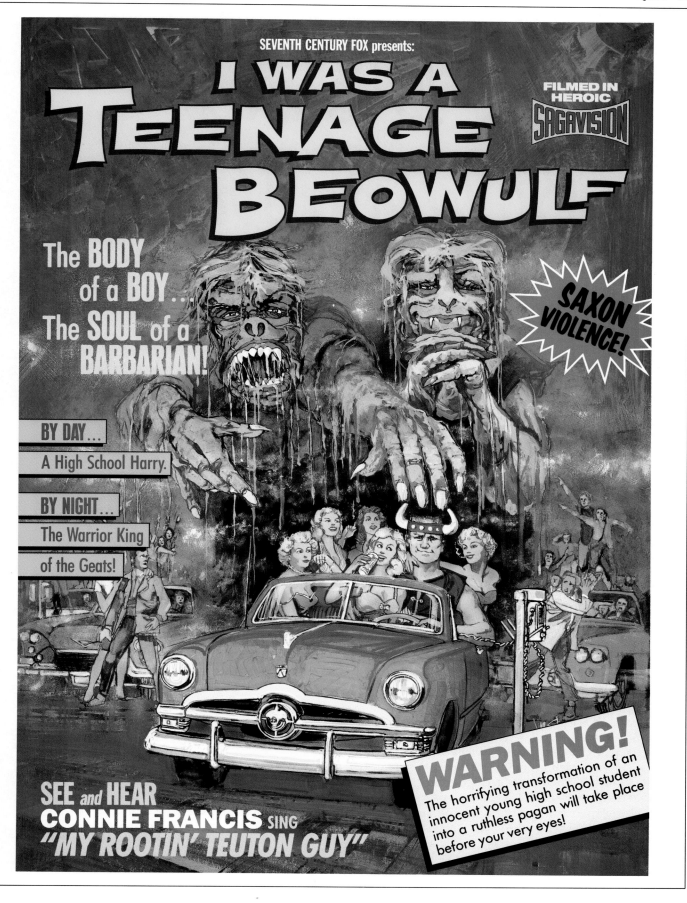

The Big Fat Balding Prince

In 1986, near the isolated mountain village of St. Affrique in southern France, a shepherd named Fabrice Mazin came upon quite a treasure. Wedged in the rocks was a military-issue aviator's emergency kit, its contents undisturbed, with an inner label clearly identifying it as having belonged to the beloved author Antoine de Saint-Exupéry, who took off in his reconaissance plane in July 1944 and was never seen again. Nestled among the supplies was a complete handwritten manuscript, the sequel to the missing writer's classic children's book *The Little Prince*. We think this charming new work leaves no doubt that the writing talents of dear "St. Ex" were equaled only by his skill as a pilot.

I

"If you please—draw me a chain saw!"

The heavy, perspiring man stood before me like an apparition on the empty Arizona highway.

"What!" I jumped, ducking my head out from under the hood of my car in astonishment. I rubbed my burning eyes in wonder at the sight of him, for I had once again broken down a hundred miles from any human habitation, having forgotten, as childlike grown-ups often do, to put gasoline in the tank.

My fuel gauge looked like this:

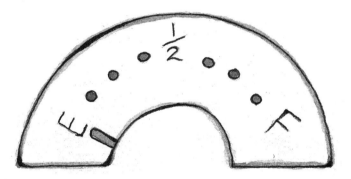

But of what use, I thought, is a gauge that tells one with symbols what can be easily felt? The car shudders, it stops, it is out of gas. I have learned much from my many years as an airplane pilot. When one's airplane is hurtling out of control toward the earth, as mine frequently did, one does not need to consult an altimeter. One knows when one must kiss one's ass goodbye. But that is another lesson.

"Draw me a chain saw!" the bedraggled fat man repeated in a voice husky with emotion, and it was then that I recognized my special friend of forty years past, a little prince who did not like to answer questions but from whom I had learned all things of any importance.

"*Now,* you idiot!" he sobbed, and he fell to his knees with his distraught face in his hands.

Yes, it was he.

And so I renewed my acquaintance with . . . the big fat balding prince.

II

In great haste I attempted to draw a chain saw for my old friend, but I had never before drawn one and I could not make it look right. Then I had an idea.

"Here," I said when I had finished. "It is a brand-new chain saw in a box."

This is very much like the drawing I gave to him:

Now, perhaps you are wondering, "Why did he lie to the big fat balding prince?" For you and I both know that there can be nothing inside a drawing of a chain-saw box. How absurd that would be!

But I recalled very well how the prince, when little, had been fooled by a drawing of a sheep inside a crate. So, I waited for his reaction.

His scowl was immediate and fierce. He looked up from the drawing as though seeing me clearly for the first time, and I knew he now remembered me.

"You!" he cried, and his red face grew redder. "It is you! You who gave me a picture of an empty goddamn box when I desperately needed a sheep! Of all the rotten, stinking luck, I had to run into *you!* Oh, ho, ho, this is funny!" he laughed, but his laughter was as hollow and hard as nails shaken in a can, and I knew that it was not funny to the big fat balding prince, not at all.

One thing that I have learned is that telling the truth is always best, especially when one can think of nothing better.

"Yes," I said sheepishly, if you will forgive the pun, though no pun was intended in the original French. "It is I. But tell me . . . little . . . prince. What has happened on your planet? Why are you here? I am very sorry about the sheep thing. But please, let me help you! I shall do better this time!"

"Tell me," the prince said abruptly. "Can I buy dynamite without a permit?"

He had not answered my questions, and I knew that he never would, a habit I did not find nearly as endearing now as I did when he was a child. But then, I hate grown-ups, and the big fat balding prince was suddenly no exception.

"*Dynamite?* Why would you possibly need such a thing! Or a chain saw!"

And then I remembered the baobabs.

Look, children, at the frightful picture of the enormous strangling baobab plants in my first book, for it was a very detailed and difficult drawing that I do not want to attempt again.

Perhaps, I thought, without the grazing sheep that he had needed to keep the baobabs from growing out of control, the prince's tiny planet had been torn asunder by their mighty roots! Just as he had feared!

"The bitch won't know what hit her!" the prince cackled, a wild gleam in his eye. "*Blooey!!* Ha ha ha!"

The bitch? About whom could he be speaking?

Over the course of the next two days, in maddeningly cryptic non sequiturs and oblique references and finally in simple statements, the big fat balding prince told me his tale.

III

He wanted to kill his rose! Not just his rose any longer, but rose *bush,* his once beloved flower having grown to lusty proportions. He wanted to kill his rose . . .

"I should have seen it from the beginning. She's nothing but a shrew!" he moaned as night fell once again. We sat on my car, eating Triscuits by the light of my last emergency flare. "A castrating harridan, a ball and chain, a monster! And when I get back there . . ." he gazed up at the starry sky dreamily, ". . . she's dead meat." He heaved a sigh. "Draw me a cigarette."

"I do not have to draw you a cigarette," I snapped impatiently. "I *have* a cigarette. Here is an actual cigarette."

I confess I was growing irritated with the big fat balding prince.

Would help never come? Soon there would be no more Triscuits. The prince could really put them away.

"She stole my youth!" the prince continued bitterly. "When I think what I might have been! You cannot imagine the loneliness, the despair, the dreadful sameness of my days. Rise . . . eat . . . clean the volcanoes . . . pull a few baobabs . . . eat . . . maybe catch a couple of sunsets . . . eat . . . go to bed! And each day seeing no one but her, tending constantly to her, listening endlessly to her, her, her!"

"Was she not grateful that you returned to her?" I asked.

I was getting very upset by the things the big fat balding prince was telling me. His love for a rose had taught me how to love, his touching belief had taught me to believe. And believing makes it so! *What is essential is invisible to the eye.* A fox came up with this, believe it or not. I quote it often to my editor and my accountant.

"Grateful! Ha!" snorted the prince. "She mocked me! 'Couldn't hack it out there, Princie?' she would say . . . And the nagging! Little by little, she completely destroyed my self-respect. 'Grow up, fatso! Why don't you get out and do something with your life? Why don't you ever meet somebody nice and invite her over like a normal person? Maybe if you got rid of that ridiculous playsuit and got yourself a decent sports jacket! Look at you! You're a loser! Taking care of me is just an excuse! You'd never make it on a planet any bigger than a two-car garage and you know it!' ''

Now, one thing I must tell you. The rose had made a convincing point. The man who sat beside me bore not a trace of the magical wisdom possessed by the boy he once was. Or the innocence. Or good looks.

Here, then, is a great mystery. For you who also loved the little prince, nothing in the universe could be the same if somewhere, we do not know where, a prince that we no longer liked had—yes or no?—murdered a rose bush . . .

You would ask yourselves: Is it yes or no? Has the big fat balding prince killed the rose bush? And you would see, if you are at all sensitive, that this is a matter of so much importance!

''Draw me a steak sandwich,'' the prince whined. ''And then draw me a machete, and then I'm getting the hell out of here.''

And I began to draw.

IV

Soon I was saved. The state trooper who rescued me was surprised to find me not just alive, but exhilarated. I told him, ''It is the heat.''

Three years have gone by . . . I have never yet told this story. But many times I have looked up at the stars, and laughed. Ah, rose! I know you are happy!

Whenever I meet someone new, I show them the drawing I made that night. It looks like this:

''Oh!'' they always say. ''That is a very nice picture of a hat!''

And I smile, and say thank-you, and we then speak of grown-up, sensible things, like fuel gauges.

But someday, somewhere, perhaps I will meet a special someone—a child, or a grown-up very like one—who understands my drawing. They will say:

''Why, that is a picture of a boa constrictor digesting a big fat balding prince!''

And they will be right.

The March 1990 auction in London of the papers of a bankrupt men's club produced a literary surprise—a trove of Rudyard Kipling memorabilia, including this previously unknown sequel, of uncertain origin, to The Man Who Would Be King.

The Man Who Would Be Queen

Since the first tribes went to war, there 'as been esprit
    de corps
Among fightin' men that's more than merely tribal;
Them Greeks that breached the gates of Troy were
    truly Mates,
And there's Jonathan and David in the Bible;
It's tradition in the ranks to protect each other's flanks
Like the Roman legions done it by the Tiber;
But you've never known the charms of the fellowship
    of arms,
Until you've 'ad it up the bloomin' Khyber!
    Up the Khyber, up the Khyber,
    It's a man's world up the Khyber,
    They'll find out if you can take it
    Up the Khyber!

"**D**amn queer country, Injah!" quoth the Semi-Retired Far East Correspondent, to the awful despair of the Subaltern he'd cornered. Moments before, said Subaltern had been carelessly jesting among a crowd of his peers, as they strolled from the mess table toward the billiards room. The Semi-Retired Far East Correspondent had cut him out of the herd as cunningly as a hungry old jackal pounces on a trailing sambur fawn.

"Oh, quite," assented the Subaltern, "yes, rather." The Semi-Retired Far East Correspondent, whom we shall henceforth call "Old Ruddy," as did all the members behind his back, was a monologist of singular persistence, and was alleged to be, as the Regimental wag punningly put it, "The Greatest Boer this side of the Transvaal." His victim, the Subaltern, knew he was in for an evening-long anecdote, complete with cockney and native

dialects, about the Struggle for Empire Somewhere East of Suez, unless he could effect a quick escape. He attempted a desperate opening stratagem: a change of subject.

"I say, old man, I've been meaning to ask you: What do you make of this business about allowing lady visitors into the Hallowed Confines? Bit of a rum go, what?"

There had, indeed, been a motion put forward by a cabal of Sandhurst Bolshies to admit members of the gentle sex to the Mess for dinner on special occasions, such as Victoria Day. The Subaltern hoped Old Ruddy would express a few platitudes of Tory indignation with which he himself could heartily agree, while slithering away to rejoin his chums.

But Old Ruddy outfoxed him. "I can't see how there can be any objection," said he, "seeing as how we've already got a lady as a member—and not only a lady, but a Queen!"

"What? I can't . . . I don't . . . surely not . . . *how*? And in Gawd's name, *who*?" stammered the Subaltern, thereby stumbling right into the trap.

"All in good time," quoth Old Ruddy. "It's rather a longish tale. Take a pew." The forlorn Subaltern collapsed into an armchair, while his captor summoned brandy and sodas from a passing mess boy, fired up a malodorous cheroot, and rumbled dramatically:

"It began in Simla, on the last day of July; which is to say, on the hottest day of the hottest month in the hottest hell-hole in all the Raj.

"Of course, cholera was rampant in camp. The hills 'round the place were teeming with hostile Sepoys, our own Ghurkas were murmuring mutinously, and supplies were short. Although I myself had a touch of fever, I knew my duty, and was at the telegraph, cabling patriotic light verse to my London publishers, when he appeared, as if by magic, before me. He had a way of doing that: creeping about, silent as a snake, and all but invisible, even in broad daylight. He was a spy, you see. Claimed he'd been trained as a child in the sinister Eastern art of sneaking up on a fellow.

"Now, don't misunderstand. The lad was no wog. He was as white as you or I; almost certainly English, or at the very worst Irish. And that was why, on this occasion, I failed at first to recognize him when he materialized before me. For his face was a reddish brown, altogether the color of a good strong cup of tea (he had, in fact, stained it that hue by means of tea leaves), and he was dressed in a flowing green and gold *sari* decorated with beads and spangles after the manner of the native females who follow after armies on the march as eagerly and inevitably as pariah dogs follow a goat-butcher's cart.

"He was affecting this unorthodox garb, he explained, as a disguise. He intended to slip out of camp at dusk, and thus avoid the gruesome doom which would that very night befall the garrison.

"I needn't tell you, I was shocked. 'Go willful-missing? Hardly *pukka*, old son,' said I to him. 'You may have been raised in the bush by some monkey-faced *guru,* but remember by Gawd you're a serving British officer now!' And I meant it to sting.

"But I must confess that his rationale for deserting, as he laid it out for me, had a certain brutal logic. He'd been up in the hills the night before, skulking noiselessly about on one of his scouting missions, and discovered that the rebellious natives were far more numerous than we had been led to believe; that they intended to attack in force, and soon; and that furthermore, some of them were actually in possession of rifles!

"Because I'd taken an interest in the lad, and actually written up the curious story of his early life in a 'human interest' series for the *Times*, he'd come to offer me a chance to escape, with him, the grisly fate awaiting our brave comrades. Naturally, I rejected as cowardly, unethical and un-British my would-be rescuer's scheme. Besides, the *sari* he had brought for my get-away disguise was sizes too large, and of a vulgar and unbecoming pattern. But for auld lang syne, and because he was a brother Mason, I wished

him Gawd speed, and he forthwith vanished as suddenly and silently as he had appeared.

"Perhaps you've heard tell of the scrimmage that took place that night on Jakko Hill between the Princess Hoffman-Hohenzolleren's Clydeside Own Royal Loyal Welterweight Huzzars, Regimental District 1099, and all the dusky, screamin' dervish devils of the Punjab. You may even have read my own stirring account of that battle, in my bestselling book, *Jingo Doggerel Ditties.*"

And now, to the supreme embarassment of the Subaltern, whose young friends were peeking 'round the door of the billiards room, pointing rudely in his direction and snickering at his discomfort, Old Ruddy began to recite from memory:

> *"O, the 'eathens of the 'indu Kush*
> *They stank like a 'erd o' goats,*
> *And when they weren't grovelin' at our boots,*
> *They was slashin' at our throats.*
> *We'd come to teach 'em the Rule of Law*
> *But for all the thanks we got,*
> *We might 'ave been dealin' with Micks or Spics*
> *Or the bone-brained 'ottentot.*
> *An' 'alf the time they was 'umble an' meek*
> *An' 'alf the time they was snooty,*
> *So we shot 'em down like a pack o' curs,*
> *As is a soldier's dooty,*
> *And we shouted in battle frenzy*
> *Through lips that were flecked with foam,*
> *'If you don't like it in Injah,*
> *Why don't you go bloody 'ome?'*

"The morning after our glorious victory, as I wandered the smoking, reeking plain strewn with Sepoy dead, shooing off the vultures and searching for souvenirs, I saw no sign of the young deserter, and I confess I never gave another thought as to what had become of him."

At this juncture, Old Ruddy paused to summon fresh drinks from the white-jacketed mess boy. "Hi! Slippy hitherao! Whiskey, get it! Panee lao!" he howled. The Subaltern rose stealthily from his seat, determined to make a break for it, but the Venerable Spinner of Tales twigged, and thrust him, with surprising strength, back into the armchair.

"Wait," he growled. "You haven't heard the half of it."

"I was afraid of that," mumbled the Subaltern.

"And days and nights went by, and the seasons changed, and the sun spun 'round the earth, or is it the other way around? I was never much for science. And in the fullness of time, I found myself, grown older and wiser if no richer, boarding a steamer in Bombay for the long voyage home.

"The 'All Ashore' had been given, and as I stood on deck, meditatively firing up a cheroot not unlike this one here, and gazing for a last time at that land, that rancid, fetid, squalid Crown Jewel of our Empire, Injah, I could hardly help noticing a great hullabaloo at the dockside.

"With a great banging of gongs and blowing of horns, and amidst a throng of brilliantly uniformed retainers, a richly appointed elephant was making its stately way toward the gangplank. The retainers performed a frenzy of whimpering prostrations as the lordly beast's still more lordly riders dismounted and proceeded to make their way aboard our vessel.

"A knowledgeable shipmate beside me at the rail soon satisfied my curiosity as to the identity of our exotic fellow passengers: 'Well, I'll be blowed! If it ain't 'is Royal bloomin' Majesty, the Maharajah of Nasalmistan an' 'is blushin' bride, off on their bleedin' 'oneymoon to Blighty!'

"The ruler of that obscure and savage principality —to white men only a name and a blank space above Nepal on the ordnance map—was, as might be expected, a swarthy, stocky, hairy brute. His bride, her face veiled in *purdah*, walked the customary ten paces behind him. She was supple and slender, and although she kept her head demurely bowed, appeared to be a good twelve inches taller than her Lord and Master. Without a doubt, these eyes— journalist's eyes, poet's eyes, novelist's and short story author's eyes—augmented by a pair of powerful British-made rimless spectacles—were the only ones in all the world which could have identified the Rajah's consort as the young officer from Simla, the very man who'd deserted the night before the Battle of Jakko Hill!

"It has always been my experience that a devil-may-care spirit of democracy prevails aboard ship, especially aboard any ship bound out of the infernal tropic regions and destined towards that earthly Eden, England. It is a heartening sight: people of all classes, castes, and stations in life may mingle quite amiably; provided, of course, one sticks to one's own deck.

"I therefore committed no offense against protocol by taking the liberty of introducing myself to the Prince and Princess of Nasalmistan during the Captain's champagne reception on our first evening at sea. I gave a ritual *salaam* to the swarthy potentate, then seized his bride's hand and applied the secret Masonic handshake. Above the *purdah* veil his eyes widened with panic, as he recognized his old messmate, and knew that I was on to his game. But he quickly recovered his composure, turned demurely to the Maharajah, and in a fluting falsetto innocently requested His Majesty's permission to have 'a few moments' private, educational conversation with the famous and learned British writer *sahib*.' The dusky despot assented, and with a great show of nonchalance (though I was fairly quivering with curiosity), I undertook a chatty stroll about the deck with the Princess of Nasalmistan.

"No sooner were we out of earshot than my friend dropped all pretense of femininity, and began to plead with me, much as a high-spirited schoolboy whose larking pranks have landed him squarely in the mulligatawny might appeal for mercy to the Prefect of Discipline. He begged me, firstly, not to reveal his true identity or gender. But with even more desperation, he implored my advice, 'as a man of the world, and on the Square, and for the sake of my mother, *Brother*, if you take my meaning.'

"As I needn't tell you, no loyal member of the Mysterious Ancient Fraternal Order can refuse such a request for help from a fellow Mason in distress, so I agreed to hear him out.

"'Brother Ruddy,' he moaned, 'that curry-eating lump of depravity back there, His Royal bloomin' Majesty, that is, expects me to *sleep* with him tonight! Oh, he's got this enormous bleedin' harem, hundreds of wives and concubines, all for to satisfy his beastly carnal desires, back home at the palace—where yours truly has been living in the lap—quite literally—of luxury for many a day and night. But for reasons I haven't now got the time to explain, I, your long lost Lodge Brother and comrade in arms, have become his choice as Number One Wife, and the blighter has taken me aboard this here ship, for to have his wicked way with me, and Brother, I'm afraid *tonight's the night*!'"

While I couldn't help reflecting that the fellow was being justly, if belatedly, served out for his cowardly dereliction of a British soldier's duty, I confess I was enormously curious to hear his account of the adventures which had led him into these extraordinary straits. I thought there might be a book or two in 'em. So I made him an offer. During our voyage, he would recount to me, in detail, everything that had befallen him since we'd parted company at Simla, and in return I would counsel him on the arcane techniques of living with a man, as a female, without ever having to perform the distasteful Rites of Venus; that is to say, I would teach him to act like a proper English wife. To this end, I pressed upon him a copy of my most recent work: the distaff version, so to speak, of my celebrated poem, 'If':

> *If you can fix your hair when all about you*
> *Are tearing theirs out, blaming it on you;*
> *If you can tell him he can go without you,*
> *Then pout, because you wanted to go, too;*
> *If you can wink, and sigh, and be vivacious,*
> *And paint your lips and eyes and scent your bust,*
> *And after acting utterly flirtatious,*
> *Take great offense at man's unseemly lust;*
>
> *If you can dress in feathers, fur, and leather*
> *While swooning over kittens, fawns, and chicks;*
> *If you can never quite remember whether*
> *A half a dozen is the same as six;*
> *If you confuse 'withdrawal' with 'deposit'*
> *When dealing with the bank account you share,*
> *If you can shop for clothes and fill your closet,*
> *And never have a decent thing to wear,*
>
> *If you can picket, bluster, march, and bellow*
> *For equal rights—protest and suffragette it—*
> *Demanding the same treatment as a fellow,*
> *Then wail and weep and blubber when you get it;*
> *If you can fill with guilt the hearts of spouses*
> *For everything they've done—or haven't done*
> *You'll wind up with both town and country houses,*
> *And—which is more—you'll be a WOMAN, son!*

"In short, the pith of my counsel to my young friend was that every night, when his favors were solicited by his husband, that insalubrious nabob, he should feign a splitting headache; and I assured him that his secret was safe with me so long as he met with me every morning, and recounted to me the Plain Tales of his picaresque exploits in the Hills. This bargain struck, we rejoined, as decorum demanded, the festivities.''

Although the Subaltern was, by means of many strong whiskeys, now passing into the third stage of drunkenness, he sensed what Old Ruddy was up to: his infamous *Scheherezade* narrative technique, the story within a story within a story. As Theseus in the labyrinth long ago had held on for dear life to Ariadne's ball of twine, he clutched mentally at the premise of this convoluted plot; if he could stay awake, he would eventually discover which of his fellow officers had once passed himself off as a colonial Queen.

Inexorably, Old Ruddy rumbled on.

"We had excellent weather on that crossing, calm seas and a cooling breeze. Each day, for several hours before *tiffin*, the transvestite Maharini and I would meet on deck, upon the pretext that I was instructing her Majesty in the language and manners of the English. It was I, however, who was taking copious notes, as my young friend described in great detail the exotic places he had visited, the bizarre characters he had met in his travels, and how he had come to be in this particular pickle.

"**E**very son of Adam who has toiled beneath the blazing Indian sun has heard tell of King Solomon's Ring: that band of richest gold in which is set a ruby of fabulous size and perfect purity, which in Biblical times the Wisest of Mortal Monarchs bestowed, in a fit of uncharacteristic lovesick folly, upon his paramour, the Queen of Sheba. According to legend, this most wonderful of baubles made its way down the centuries and generations, and across the seas, to the remote Kingdom of Nasalmistan, whose dynastic ruler is wont, even in our day, to bestow it upon his favorite wife. In his lust to possess the Ring of Solomon, my young friend had journeyed many a hard mile, and then, with many a maidenly wile, won the heart of the Maharajah. The Ring, he told me, was, even as we spoke, nearby: in his odious husband's richly appointed stateroom, by his bedside. He had endured much and suffered long to gain that invaluable trinket; and yet now he hesitated, understandably loath to pay its final price!''

The weary Subaltern struggled to stay awake, or at least to remain partially on the surface of consciousness, as a drowning man fights against the relentless undertow of the Bay of Bengal. There were already too many characters, flashbacks, dialects, subplots, and bits of local color in this tale. Really, it was too wicked of Old Ruddy to suddenly introduce this (however typical) Rosicrucian mystical-anthropological business of "Solomon's Ring" at this point in the narrative! But the Tale Teller nudged him sharply in the ribs, and his eyes twinkled behind his specs, as if to say, 'Now we're getting to the juicy part . . .'

"Now it happened that during these daily rambles about the ship, my young friend would frequently stop, and gaze with a good deal of interest, and more than a touch of envy, at one of our fellow passengers: a strapping lad who wore the resplendent dress uniform of a lieutenant colonel of the Bengal Lancers. 'Look at that chap there,' he'd wistfully say, 'a bleedin' hero on his way back home from the wars, destined, no doubt, for acclaim and success in his particular line o' work! He's about my age and shape and size, ain't he, brother? I could be him, and he could be me, but for an ironical twist o' fate, of the type so popular with you late-nineteenth-century authors.''

"And little did I know, or suspect, what role that officer would play in the tragedy—or was it a comedy?—about to unfold!

"By and by, we drew near to Brittania's dear shores, until it was our last evening at sea. The Captain laid on a bit of a do, with music and dancing and what not, during which the enchantingly gowned and sensuously scented pseudo-Maharini flirted most outrageously with the handsome Lancer, suggesting to him a midnight assignation on the afterdeck; nor was there any doubt that the suspicious and jealous Maharajah himself was within earshot of their nefarious scheming; but for myself, after joining the ship's company in numerous rum-punch toasts to Injah, England, and the Empire, I trundled innocently off to my cabin and my welcoming berth.

"Sometime before dawn, I was wrested from sleep by the galvanizing clanging of the ship's bell, and vigorous shouts of 'Man overboard!' I dressed hastily, and dashed out onto the deck to play an Englishman's part in whatever rescue drill was on. The ship, of course, had come to a full stop, and wallowed on the calm and greasy waters, caught square in the beam of the full moon, which had drooped to the very horizon. Off the starboard side, tossing on the waves with ironic, glittering gaudiness, were the bejeweled dress turban and gossamer peacock colored *sari* of the Maharajah and Princess of Nasalmistan; of their honorable corporeal selves, the most diligent search could discover nary a trace.

"An hour behind schedule, and two passengers short of a load, we disembarked the following afternoon, and a strangely subdued homecoming it was. Our joy at setting foot upon our native shore was naturally tempered with sorrow for the deaths, suicidal though they may have been, of the royal colonial bride and groom.

"In a blessed English drizzle, we descended in silence to the pier; among us, the handsome young Bengal Lancer. His smart scarlet uniform appeared to fit him rather loosely; under his hairline and about his wrists and neck there were traces of what appeared to be tea-stains; and from his hand flashed— a ruby ring of preternatural magnificence!

"And so the wheel of *karma* turns, and turns once more. An English lad, born in the Raj, raised up in the ranks, suffers 'outrageous fortune's slings and arrows,' and is in his time a rich man and a poor man, beggar and thief. He endures the ebb and flow of the tides of *kismet*; he is a hero, and a coward, and a hero again; a man, and a woman, and a man again. And now, young fellow, I ask you to hazard a guess. Have you surmised which member of our Club was—or is— the Man Who Would Be Queen?"

There were, in fact, at this late hour, only the two of them left in the Club; Old Ruddy and the soundly, profoundly sleeping Subaltern. With a half smile and a philosophic shrug—this had happened to him many times before—the Semi-Retired Far East Correspondent arose, and made for the door. As he did so, he tucked back into his watchfob pocket the prop he had expected to reveal as the punch line, so to speak, of his story—a ruby ring with a sinister gleam, gaudy and enormous as a carbuncle. And he hummed softly to himself:

Oh the Africans and Asians
Are a burden for Caucasians,
And although miscegenation is a sin,
From Mandalay to Siam,
You're a better man than I am,
But I'm the better woman, Gunga Din!

If you're the type of serious reader who wishes Doctor Faustus had been a podiatrist, this is the club for you!

Save $113.90 and enjoy a spellbinding welcome to The Library of Yiddish Sequels.

Do you remember the moment you opened *Moby-Dick* for the first time? Within moments you were swept away by the awesome power of Melville's narrative, enthralled by his meticulous descriptions of nineteenth-century maritime life, and deeply moved by his evocative portraits of Ishmael, Ahab, and of course, Moby himself. But, truthfully now—wouldn't you have enjoyed the book even more if the whale had been Jewish?

And how about Charles Dickens's *A Christmas Carol*? The story: logical and fascinating. The characterizations: penetrating and memorable. The moral: a message of universal meaning and importance for all humankind. But can a non-Christian child—or adult—*really* relate to it?

"One of the Boldest Publishing Programs Ever"

It was penetrating questions like these that motivated the Yiddish-American Heritage Society to inaugurate one of the boldest publishing programs ever undertaken: the Library of Yiddish Sequels. Each month we prepare a new sequel to a classic work of Gentile literature: a sequel whose plot, setting, and principal characters have been converted, so to speak, so that Yiddish-Americans can feel truly comfortable with them.

Right now, you can acquire any three of these astonishing works for a combined price of only $5.95 (a single volume regularly retails for $39.95!). This purchase alone makes you a lifetime member of the Yiddish-American Heritage Society and automatically entitles you to buy additional volumes at our subscriber's discounts (as much as 29%).

Books of Uncommon Beauty and Durability

And what magnificent volumes they are: with individually designed bindings of natural cloth, crushed velour, or Corinthian leather (specify which you prefer), the very finest quality of paper, and special protective slipcovers that will keep your editions dust-free and beautiful, even after many years on the shelf.

Membership Has Its Additional Pleasures

The Yiddish-American Heritage Society is much more than just a book club. The Society has a Reading Gallery on Manhattan's fashionable Upper West Side (see the accompanying illustration) where members may browse in luxurious surroundings through any volume in our ever-growing Library. We also organize annual literary debates—past speakers have included Harry Golden, Sam Levenson, and Allan Sherman.

How to Start Building Your Own Library of Yiddish Sequels

Why shouldn't you join today? Select any three of the magnificent sequels on the partial list below (less than 5% of our entire collection!), fill out the coupon, place it in an envelope with your check or money order, and deposit it in the mail. Within a few days, you'll receive your books, a handsome membership card, and a prospectus listing the more than 1,000 incomparable volumes you'll be able to possess at our remarkable discounts.

LYS

The Library of Yiddish Sequels
A Project of the Yiddish-American Heritage Society
New York, New York

Yes, please send me the three books I have checked off below—and enroll me as a lifetime member of the Yiddish-American Heritage Society—for $5.95 (total pub. price $119.85). I understand that my membership privileges include the unlimited right to use the Society's Reading Gallery and permits me to acquire additional handsome, durable sequels at close-to-wholesale prices.

___The Accidental Tsuris
___The Autobiography of Alice B. Tochis
___The Big Shlep
___The Blintz and the Pauper
___Brave World, Nu?
___The Bris of San Luis Rey
___The Brothers Karamazeltov
___Bupkes Before Dying
___The Catcher on Rye
___Come Back, Little Shivah
___A Cool Minyan
___A Coupla Boychiks Sittin' Around Talkin'
___The Crying of Latke 49
___Doctor Shekel and Mr. Hyde
___The Dreck of the Hesperus
___Dybbuk of Laughter and Forgetting
___The Electric Kool-Aid Hasid Test
___Fanny Hillel

___Gonif with the Wind
___Good Bar Mitzvah Chips
___The Heart of the Shmatte
___How They Brought the Good Noodge from Ghent to Aix
___In Cold Borscht
___Jonathan Livingston Siegal
___Katz' Dreidl
___Kishka Me Deadly
___Klutz Encounters of the Third Kind
___The Kugel Has Landed
___Kvetch-22
___Leda and the Shlong
___Litvak in Anger
___Lubliners
___The Maltese Flanken
___Matzoh Do About Nothing
___Megillahs in the Mist
___Mensch of La Mancha

___Meshuggahland Express
___A Midsummer Night's Derma
___Moyl Flanders
___My Shiksa Eileen
___Oy Vay Atque Vale
___Oy, Wilderness!
___A Perfect Day for Gefilte Fish
___The Prisoner of Zelda
___The Putzman Always Rings Twice
___Rabbi Run
___The Rape of the Lox
___Remembrance of Things Plotzed
___She Shtups to Conquer
___A Shlockwork Orange
___Shlong of Shlongs

___A Shlump Unto My Feet
___The Shmaltz of the Toreadors
___The Shmooze of the Pisher Man
___The Shmuck of Roaring Camp
___A Shtarker Is Born
___Shvantz Way
___Stopping By Woods on a Shmoey Evening
___To Have and Have Nosh
___To His Goy Mistress
___To Kvell a Macherbird
___A Tush of the Poet
___Two Gentile Men of Verona
___Two Shmeers Before the Mast
___The Voyage of the Bagel
___A Yenta Mental Journey
___The Zaftig Machine

I prefer my volumes to be bound in
___ natural cloth   ___ crushed velour   ___ Corinthian leather

I am enclosing a   ___ personal check   ___ money order for $5.95.

Name _____

Address _____

City _____

State _____ Zip code _____

Brideshead Revisited Revisited

Millions of readers of Evelyn Waugh's Brideshead Revisited *and tens of millions of viewers of the British television miniseries have long demanded to know what became of Charles Ryder and the surviving members of the Marchmain family in the years following World War II. Here, at last, is the Epi-epilogue of the novel.*

Although Evelyn Waugh was not opposed to sequels as such (in fact, he wrote a trilogy and was fond of running characters) he inexplicably failed to produce a follow-up to *Brideshead Revisited.*

There is some evidence, however, that he once considered writing a prequel covering the younger years of Lord and Lady Marchmain tentatively titled *Brideshead Previsited.*

"**W**e're here, Sir Charles," said my chauffeur.

I had dozed off again in the back of the Rolls, and it required an effort for me to bring to mind exactly which "here" the chauffeur was referring to. The most awkward thing about old age—and I mean *antiquity,* for I am eighty-five this year—is the perpetual disorientation. It is rather like the problem one encounters when one has two households, an establishment in town one occupies during the week and a place in the country to which one repairs at the weekends, and one is forever reaching into writing desks and opening cupboards in a petulant search for things one knows perfectly well were put there only yesterday, when, of course, they reside in a drawer or on a shelf a full forty miles away.

And yet it is so much worse, for after one has lived as long as I have, past events are no longer neatly arranged, one after the other, like familiar stations along the railway line taken each week to and from the city. They are hopelessly jumbled up or missing entirely, and some unspeakable tea-time one had to endure at the age of eleven with a frightful aunt who had a moustache and a mole on her chin the size of a biscuit is what one minutely recollects, as if it happened yesterday—and often instead of whatever *did* happen yesterday—while having breakfast one morning nine hundred months later. It is like being a permanent visitor in some ill-lit foreign museum with a baffling layout, no maps, and sullen guards who speak a language with too many vowels, in which one stumbles from room to room, passing directly from ancient Egypt, to nineteenth-century France, to classical Rome, to the Quattrocento, finally emerging, bewildered and vexed, into a bright entrance hall where unshaven students in ragged pullovers are examining with numb earnestness a misshapen heap of slag fashioned from scrap metal by some narcotized moron with a blowtorch.

I looked out of the car window just as we passed through the wrought-iron gates framed on either side by the sober Grecian symmetry of the lodges. I remembered clearly that June day I had first laid eyes upon them, more than half a century ear-

THE BOOK OF SEQUELS

lier, when Sebastian Flyte and I had driven down from Oxford in Hardcastle's motor during Eights Week, but I could not for the life of me fathom why I had returned to Brideshead today.

"Crimmins," I said, "What the devil am I doing back here again?" I had long since given up any attempt to disguise my failing memory with sly, circuitous attempts to fill in the sudden blank spots with oblique inquiries and offhand requests for some tidbits of information that might illuminate the vast, dark spaces of forgetfulness, like the coins you put in the little box in Italian churches to light up the frescoes for a minute.

"It's *Cummings,* sir," my long-suffering chauffeur politely insisted. "We've come for the dedication of the Ryder Room. There will be the wallahs from the National Trust, one or two light-footed lads from the Royal Academy, the R.C. Bishop of Birmingham, the Duchess of Shropshire, and the local dignitaries." He ticked off the high points like a practised advance man for a politician, which was precisely what he had been until a minister in his charge had been surprised *in flagrante* with a seamstress whom the *Daily Slur* alleged to have a Soviet connection with the headline, WAS IT A HEMMER AND SICKLE AFFAIR?

I began to recall the reason for my journey. The Trust had taken it in their wooly heads to bring back to a glory they never possessed the painfully amateurish landscapes with which I had despoiled the walls of a little garden room at Brideshead over the course of many visits to the Marchmain household during the Thirties.

But no sooner had I thus established myself in the present than the sight of the great park filled with oaks and limes and beeches and the distant dome of the house instantly transported me back to the last time I had seen this view, when I was Captain Ryder and my Brigade had briefly been billetted here, in the spring of 1944, and as we drove up towards the front of the house where the great fountain stood, I no-

ticed with alarm the long rows of Mercedes coaches and the milling hordes—the solemn masses of dumpling-headed Germans and the troops of Japanese bobbing and chittering like macaques.

"Sergeant Cummings!" I shouted. "Form the men up double quick! The bloody Huns and Nips have invaded! Send a runner to headquarters! Where's my kit?" Cummings brought the car to a stop in one of the side courts and helped to extricate me from its constricted interior. Rolls-Royce, indeed—the modern models are glorified Fords with a peculiar radiator and a tin statue on the bonnet.

A slim young man from the National Trust stepped forward, introduced himself, and helped me up the stairs. "We are so very honored to have you with us here today, Sir Charles," he said, in a languid voice whose smooth tones could have been sold commercially as a lubricant.

"Thank you, Cecil," I said. I had already forgotten his wretched name, but they're almost always called Cecil.

We entered the massive house and made our way towards the garden room, passing in succession through the Great

> *"Form the men up double quick! The bloody Huns and Nips have invaded! Send a runner to headquarters! Where's my kit?"*

Hall, the library, the parlor, the sitting-room, and the morning room, and except for the velvet ropes that kept the tourists' hands off the cabinetry and the rubber mats that protected the parquet floors from their deplorable footwear, Brideshead looked as fresh and resplendent as it must have done on the day, a century and a half earlier, when the architects had completed their work. All evidence of time and neglect, not to mention the sundry damages of occupation inflicted by the troops of my Brigade, had been erased through the patient labors of Lady Julia during the years right after the war.

The Castle owed its rescue to one of those rare occurrences that seem to offer to even the most dubious a truly convincing proof of God's existence. Rex Mottram, strolling home from Whitehall where his exceptionally capable wartime performance had set the stage for a brilliant postwar political career, was obliterated by the very last V-2 to fall on London, and as a consequence, the life insurance policy which he had purchased for Julia's benefit in lieu of contributing a sum in trust to match her dowry, was paid out to her, and she found herself, in a time when sterling still had some value and things had not yet become expensive, with a half a million pounds in cash, tax-free.

For a dozen years, Julia had applied herself to the task of restoring Brideshead. It was as if, having concluded in her oddly practical way that her past transgressions in the eyes of her Church prevented her from ever figuratively putting her house in order, she determined to do so in a literal sense. She pursued the work with the zeal of one who has at last found a true vocation: she cast out the rot, exorcised the

---

The Castle owed its rescue to one of those rare occurrences that offer to even the most dubious convincing proof of God's existence.

---

damp, rehabilitated the roofs, purged the chimneys, cleansed the masonry, made whole the foundations, interceded on behalf of the cellars, resurrected the gardens, and ministered to the forsaken lawns. Perhaps it was true that she could not eradicate the indelible blot of mortal sin on her soul, but she certainly could expunge the stains from the priceless old carpets and tapestries; quite possibly, she herself was beyond salvation, but she could see to the redemption of the roses; and maybe she was destined for eternal torment, but that was no reason to let the hedges go to hell.

"Julia," I said out loud suddenly, startling Cecil. The thought of her, and the

utter waste of happiness, hers and mine, caused by her morbid devotion to her family's religion, made me rap my cane on the floor in fury.

I had not spoken with her again after we parted on the day Lord Marchmain died. I would see her from time to time, of course, and we would wave or exchange nods, but there was a wall between us now, and the low door that might once have provided a passage through it was bricked over with the grey stone ashlars of the Church.

I had attended her funeral. It was held here at Brideshead in the appalling art nouveau chapel which was briefly reconsecrated for the ritual of her departure from this earth, a dreary service performed by a singularly uninspired representative of the organization that had helped make her time upon it so miserable.

Sebastian had been long dead by then—with that odd mixture of charm and sanctity that was uniquely his, he had somehow managed to die some years before on St. Sebastian's Day—but Bridey was there with the former Mrs. Muspratt (I wonder if even then he was thinking of carving her up and scattering the bits around a rubbish tip in Woking, as he did, not quite a year later), and so was Cordelia, back from interrupted good works in one of those countries in Africa with a name that sounds like something gardeners spray the fruit trees to prevent. She was as sweet and effervescent as ever, and she cheerfully informed me that Julia had left Brideshead to the National Trust, knowing full well that if it had been left to her, she would have straightaway deeded it to the Church.

By the time we reached the entrance to the garden room, there was a small crowd gathered in the large, featureless foyer that abutted it, which I discovered to my horror had now been given over to a ghastly souvenir shop which offered for sale sweatshirts stencilled with the facade of the house on one side and the legend "I Revisited Brideshead" on the other, and replicas, in three sizes, of poor Sebastian's teddy-bear, Aloysius.

"Et in Arcadio ego," I said, and then everything went black.

When I returned to consciousness I found myself in the Chinese drawing-room, laid out on the very bed that Lord Marchmain had died in fifty years earlier. It took me a minute or two to place myself in my surroundings, and for one awful moment I thought I saw myself, Charles Ryder, standing at the foot of the bed regarding me with pity, but it was only Cecil, and I quickly recognized the worthy personages who had come for the dedication and who were now preparing themselves for what they obviously believed was to be an abrupt passage from Congratulation to Mourning.

It was not to be. I have these fainting spells from time to time, but my doctor—what *is* his name?—assures me that they are unlikely ever to be fatal, though they do make me look rather like Death warmed over for an hour or so. Oddly, I always feel much better right afterwards, and for a time at least, very clearheaded.

"Is there a Catholic priest here?" I called out, in as weak a voice as I could manage. I knew perfectly well there was,

for I had spotted the Bishop whose presence Cummings had predicted in the welcoming throng. He appeared at once, and making his way to my bedside, he went right into his incantations. I feigned sleep while he muttered and dabbed, but when he got to the heart of the matter and asked if I might make some sign, however slight, of remorse for my sins, I raised my hand

---

...for one awful moment I thought I saw myself, Charles Ryder, standing at the foot of the bed, regarding me with pity....

---

with as convincing a mimickry of superhuman effort as I could muster, turned the palm at right angles to my face, placed the thumb against the tip of my nose, and then, in a gesture as timeless as the altars and temples of men, I vigorously wiggled my fingers.

"That was a very naughty thing to do, Sir Charles," said Cummings, when we were well on the road back to London.

"Mmm, quite," I said, but I didn't have the faintest idea what he was talking about.

Trees XXXIX-XLVI

More Entries from Joyce Kilmer's Notebook

*I think my pen shall never glean
A poem like a collard green...*

*I think I never shall address
A poem crisp as watercress...*

*I think that I shall never hail
A poem like a bunch of kale...*

*I think that I shall never greet
A poem smoky as mesquite...*

*I think that I have never struck a
Poem stout-stemmed as a yucca...*

*I think that I shall never heed
A poem slender as a reed...*

*I think I'll never execute
A poem like a taro root...*

*I doubt I'll find before I die a
Poem weird as a papaya...*

Answers to the Letters of
George Bernard Shaw

Although most of George Bernard Shaw's voluminous correspondence has been published over the years, only a handful of the fascinating replies to his letters survive. And as these precious examples clearly indicate, the noted playwright's unaccountable failure to preserve the responses to his wry, insightful missives was a tragic blow to Shavian scholarship.

Dear Mr Shaw:

Thank you for your inquiry of June the 12th regarding your order.

We regret to inform you that the exuberantly patterned material you selected for your waistcoat is no longer available, owing to the untimely demise of our sole supplier of the aforementioned cloth. As of yet we have been unable to locate a suitable replacement for that particular weave.

We invite you to visit our premises at your earliest convenience to make an alternate selection. And perhaps, at the same time, you may wish to examine some of the colourful silk shirtings whose recent arrival from Bombay we have the pleasure of taking this opportunity to announce.

> Yours truly,
> Andrew Hawley
> Helms & Hawley
> Bespoke Tailors
> New Bond Street
> London

Dear Mr Shaw:

We are in receipt of your missive of the 13th of March. May I say that your explicit language was found most disturbing by our Mrs Higgins, whose strict Presbyterian upbringing left her quite unprepared for the intemperance of your diatribe.

I can assure you that the African elephant's foot umbrella stand which we shipped to you left our establishment in perfect condition, and was packed in a manner which absolutely precludes the possibility of its having suffered in transit the damage which you so vividly described.

I can only surmise that the breakage of one of the animal's toenails was the direct result of the negligence of you yourself or one of your perhaps insufficiently trained household staff.

> I have the honor to remain,
> Your obedient servant,
> Horace Twickenham
> Dealer in curios and rarities
> Regent Street
> London

Dear Mr Shaw:

We are writing to inform you that the parcel addressed by you to a Mr Adam Douglass, The Larches, Oldwycke, Devonshire, has been returned to our Victoria Street office. The postage affixed to this package was insufficient in the amount of seven (7) shillings—a deficiency which Mr Douglass was either unable, or unwilling, to correct.

Payment by you of the outstanding sum will allow us to redeliver the package, or, alternatively, you may collect the parcel. Our office is open during regular business hours every day excepting Sunday.

> Sincerely yours,
> William Whaley
> Deputy Postmaster

Dear Mr Shaw:

Thank you for your most recent letter. We at the Underground Lines are always ready to hear your proposals for improvements in our service.

Although I must concede that the inclusion of "vegetarian-snack carriages" in our trains would be a welcome convenience for some of our passengers, I am very much afraid that the rather complex logistics involved make your interesting proposal somewhat impractical.

If you have any additional suggestions, we will, of course, accord them the close attention they deserve.

> As ever,
> Angus Mackenzie
> Assistant to the Director of Services
> London Underground Railways, Ltd

Dear Mr Shaw:

Following the instructions detailed in your letter of May 26th, I have made a thorough inspection of the foundations of your residence. I am sorry to have to report to you that there is evidence of moisture seepage in the masonry, and until this condition is corrected (a service which I am equipped to perform at a relatively modest expense), it would be most inadvisable to install the massive shell-studded grotto which you propose.

Incidentally, I had the occasion to notice that your basement steps have reached an advanced stage of dilapidation, and constitute a possible threat to life and limb. I would recommend their immediate replacement with a set of "Stride Right Safety Stairs," a patented prefabricated stairway system for which I have the honour of being the sole local authorised installer.

> I remain,
> Sincerely yours,
> Harold Evans
> Member, Royal Society of Engineers
> Dulwich

Dear Mr Shaw:

I am in receipt of what I take to be a misdirected letter over your signature, addressed to Miss Abigail McGinty in the town of Galway. Although Abigail McGinty *is* my name, and I do indeed reside in Galway, I am quite certain that I am not the intended audience for your rather unorthodox monograph on the misuse of dipthongs.

However, I do sense most strongly that my having been brought into the sphere of your acquaintance in this "chance" fashion cannot but reveal the presence of a force larger and stronger than ourselves.

I, too, am one possessed of passionate convictions (although mine run more to politics than phonetics), and I am emboldened by this "coincidence" to enclose, for your perusal, some literature which I have prepared in support of granting household pets the franchise.

I feel that you were destined to receive this material, just as I know that I was fated to come into possession of your home address just a week before my long-scheduled visit to London to address the Committee for Canine and Feline Suffrage.

À bientôt!

> Your "accidental" friend,
> Abbie McGinty

Everything You Wanted to Know About Sacks *

* But Were So Aphasic You Forgot to Ask

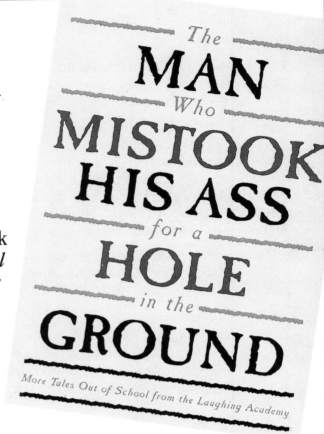

The MAN Who MISTOOK HIS ASS for a HOLE in the GROUND

More Tales Out of School from the Laughing Academy

Because Dr. Oliver Sacks's The Man Who Mistook His Wife for a Hat *was not an altogether venal and pandering work, its publisher was initially frightened and confused by its popular success. But he has now goaded the erstwhile scholarly author to create a spate of quick sequels. Following are excerpts from the most recent volume.*

In layman's terms, one might say that to be 'sane', or 'normal', is simply to know the difference between 'this here' and 'that there'. For example, many an army recruit is considered a 'stupid idiot' when unable to distinguish between the identities—and, consequently, the proper functions—of his 'rifle' and his 'gun'. And it is proverbially essential that you or I, when about to polish our boots, be able to 'tell' 'shit' from 'shinola'.

Yet it must be admitted that the behavior of persons suffering from such 'this-that' neurological disorders can be—dare one say it?—*amusing,* as when certain 'critics' are absurdly unable to distinguish between my own published works—elegant, compassionate, humanistic and best-selling anthologies of case histories—and 'another bunch of nuthouse jokes'.

Their 'sickness' is identical to that of a patient described by my mentor, the pioneer Soviet physician I. Kutchalobzoff:

While participating in a professionally-guided tour of our hospital's neurology ward, this subject became violently delusional, and began inexplicably to protest that he had been 'taken to the freak show'.

I have recently discovered and isolated a new and widespread neurological disorder which I have named 'hypertranslexia', in honor of its primary symptom, the patient's almost perverse inability to translate anything properly.

Contemplate, if you will, the case of an earlier (elegant, compassionate, humanistic, etc.) book of mine which has been issued in dozens of foreign editions, not one of which is correctly titled. What are we to make of:

- **Crazy Sahib, Him Think Wife Turban All Same!**
- **Pardon Me, Monsieur, but You Appear to Be Having Sexual Intercourse with My Beret**
- **Anyplace He Hang His Wife Is Home Sweet Home to He**
- **What an Error, to Put Mistress on His Skull!**
- **Ai, Caramba! It's the Mexican Wife Dance!**
- **How to Make Love to Your Hat**
- **That Was No Lady, That Was My Stetson!**
- **The Ten Gallon Wife**

Anyone who thinks that Germans in general, and German philosophers in particular, lack a sense of humor has never read Friedrich Nietzsche's sidesplitting—and thought-provoking—sequel to his enigmatic masterpiece,

Thus Joked Zarathustra

(Also spasst Zarathustra)

Zarathustra gathered his disciples and said to them:

You who do not fear to be assailed by enigmas, you who are intoxicated by riddles, hear me:

Why would a man of great passion but little intellect hurl his timepiece from the uppermost window of his house?

Because his heart burned with the unquenchable desire to see time fly!

And how could it be that the enlightened man does not perish of a terrible hunger after being stranded on the barren, empty beach of a desolate shore?

He is able to survive for one reason and one reason alone: seeing what the blind mob cannot, he eats greedily and with great relish the sand-which-is there!

Tell me, my brothers: when shall a door that is set in the forbidding fastness of a stone wall cease utterly to be a door?

This is the answer you seek with the pure longing of your being: such a door is no longer a door at that exalting moment when it is ajar!

And ponder this question: by what means can seven mighty elephants be accommodated in a single carriage?

The solution is easy for the Superman, whose mind is unclouded by petty fears and foolish doubts. He will not *calculate,* he will *guess!* He cries: Place three of the weighty creatures in the front seat, and four in back!

My friends, if it were possible through the working of our all-mastering wills to cross a herd of cows with a flock of ducks, what name would we give to our phantasmal creation?

Prepare your spirits for the annihilating answer: milk and quackers!

Behold! Does your empty wisdom permit you to know the world-sundering difference between a day filled with tempests and storms and a noble, wounded bull?

Overcome your ignorance as you encounter this bitter heart-piercing truth: one is pouring with rain, the other is roaring with pain!

And now solve for me one final, profound puzzle: where does the mad, bold, fierce, warlike, life-seizing 500-pound Superman sleep?

Truly, he sleeps *anywhere he wants!*

Thus joked Zarathustra.

Notes made by Nietzsche just before he went completely insane show that he struggled with the central questions of his nihilist philosophy to the very end. "For what triumphant purpose does the Superchicken cross the broad, traffic-thronged highway?" reads the final entry in his notebook. Alas, Nietzsche lost his mind before he found the answer.

The recent discovery of a happy ending to Romeo and Juliet *that bears the unmistakable mark of the master's hand and sets the stage for a sequel clearly shows that the Bard was not only England's greatest playwright, but her greatest replaywright as well.*

Romeo and Juliet
Part 1 (cont.)

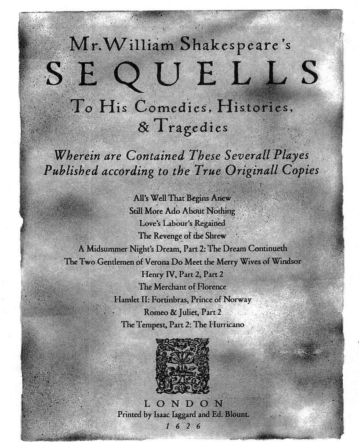

Mr. William Shakespeare's
SEQUELLS
To His Comedies, Histories, & Tragedies

Wherein are Contained These Severall Playes Published according to the True Originall Copies

All's Well That Begins Anew
Still More Ado About Nothing
Love's Labour's Regained
The Revenge of the Shrew
A Midsummer Night's Dream, Part 2: The Dream Continueth
The Two Gentlemen of Verona Do Meet the Merry Wives of Windsor
Henry IV, Part 2, Part 2
The Merchant of Florence
Hamlet II: Fortinbras, Prince of Norway
Romeo & Juliet, Part 2
The Tempest, Part 2: The Hurricano

LONDON
Printed by Isaac Iaggard and Ed. Blount.
1 6 2 6

The only surviving copy of the title page of the "Second Folio," a long-lost edition of previously unknown sequels to eleven of Shakespeare's most popular plays. This tantalizing list of vanished masterpieces was printed on one leaf of a pair of folio sheets bound by mistake into *Lordlie Larde: Ye Cooke's Delighte,* a compendium of Elizabethan recipes based on pork fat. The other misplaced pages, which were inserted after a section on "Heftie Dumplinges," contain a rewritten Act V, Scene 3, for *Romeo and Juliet* (now titled *Romeo and Juliet, Part 1*) which, if authentic, suggests that Shakespeare had come to regret his decision to dispatch the lovesick duo and resolved to bring them back for an encore.

ACT V: SC III (CONT.)

Prince. A glooming peace this morning with it brings.
The sun for sorrow will not show his head.
Go hence, to have more talk of these sad things;
Some shall be pardoned, and some punished;

For never was a story of more woe
Than this of Juliet and her Romeo.
As all begin to exit, ROMEO *arises.*
Romeo. Romeo! Who calls my name?
Montague. O, Romeo!
It is not dawn, and yet my son doth rise!
O precious chip from off this foolish block,

310

Thou art alive, or I am not thy sire,
But uncle to some monkey's hairy brood!
                         Romeo swoons.
    Prince. He speaks his name? How can this be?
    His tongue
That now his nomenclature doth proclaim
Methought as dumb and wordless in his mouth
As is its leather namesake in my shoe
Which, bound in silent service to a foot,   320
Doth mutely cap the meter of my pace.
                    FRIAR *picks up poison cup.*
    Friar. How this has come to pass I can divine,
And thus divining, see Divin'ty's hand.
The pharmacist who hath this potion sold
Perchance made timid by the awful law
That death for death's prescription doth prescribe
In place of poison put a potent draught
That causeth deepest sleep but nothing more,
And so did cheat both Romeo and Death.
Alas, in all these matters I am versed,   330
For such a compound I myself did give
To Juliet.
                         JULIET *stirs.*
    Juliet. What's this? Who summons me?
                         JULIET *swoons.*
    Capulet. Juliet! But no, it is her ghost that
    speaks,
A Juliet of the spirits, a mere shade,
Come now to castigate me.
                    FRIAR *attends* JULIET.
    Friar. God be praised!
She lives!
    Capulet. O, do not tempt me with false hopes!
I saw her bloody wound. Did my eyes lie?
My hands, when they did come upon her skin
And said, " 'Tis cold," did they prevaricate?
    Friar. The chill that lays upon her I ascribe   340
Unto my drug's effects, which shall abate.
As for the gore that carmines all her garb
It doth not look like blood. Bring nigh that torch!
                    WATCHMAN *advances.*
Aha! It is some berry's sanguine sap!
And here upon her chest there is no gash;
'Tis but the merest pinprick.
                    CAPULET'S WIFE *attends* JULIET.
    Wife. O, 'tis true!
Sweet Juliet's pallid limbs, once cold as stone
Are filled with warmth, her icy cheeks are flushed!
And like Pygmalion's marble paramour,

Through Heaven's agency she comes to life!   350
                    CAPULET *embraces his* WIFE.
    Capulet. O, my fair lady! Bless you, dearest
    wife!
Glad news of Juliet thou hast brought me twice
When she's delivered both from womb and tomb!
    Prince. I know that chemists can a physic mix
That hath the very stink of deadliness
And 'twill be mild as milk, yet where's the smith
Who can a dagger from soft feathers forge,
Or hammer stubborn steel as limp as silk?
                    BALTHASAR *picks up dagger.*
    Balthasar. My lord, this fell stiletto in my hand
Which Juliet did from Romeo's scabbard draw   360
And tried to plunge into her heavy heart
Is but a stage device, an actor's prop.
'Twas switched for my good master's golden dirk
By travelling tragedians while we slept.
We shared their camp last night upon the road
From Mantua. They played for us a piece
Called 'Murther of the Prince.'
    Prince. I've seen't. 'Tis trash.
    Balthasar. Th'assassin in it, when he stabbed his
    lord
Employed this cunning tool to mime the deed.
See here, the blade is set upon a spring   370
Concealed within the dagger's hollow hilt
Which doth contain a vial of ruby juice.
The thrust that makes the audience gasp doth drive
A dull, flat tip against the Thespian's breast
And sends the blade not forward into flesh
But back into the handle of the knife
Where by its action it propels a pump,
And sprays the player with a gush of blood
That would have made the Hun, Attila, swoon.
    Friar. No doubt it was the shock of that
    discharge   380
That sent Juliet into the deathlike faint
From which, methinks, she shortly shall arise.
                    ROMEO *awakens again.*
    Romeo. I breathe, I move, I see. Then do I live?
It canst not be! The venom in my veins
Hath brought me death, and now I am in Hell.
But what is this? Dread Hades' halls are filled
From wall to wall with fair Verona's sons.
Hath hungry Earth oped up her rocky jaws
And made a dainty morsel of our town?
Did some covert Vesuvio belch fire   390
And yield our land to Vulcan's ashy grasp?

Friar. The herbs do give you visions, Romeo.
Romeo. Good man of God, how came you to be here?
Why aren't thou settled in the other place?
                              JULIET *rises*.
Juliet. Romeo! When I pronounce those syllables
They leave a taste of honey on my lips!
   Romeo. O dearest Juliet! If thou came here
It is not Hell, because where'er thou art,
That place becomes a paradise for me!
                              They embrace.
But hold. Your raiment tells of massacre   400
Yet when I saw thee dead, no blood was on't.
   Juliet. What you beheld was not the face of death;
It was the visage of his sibling, sleep,
From whose embrace I did awake too late.
   Romeo. I quaffed a drug.
   Friar. 'Twas not a mortal brew.
   Juliet. And I thy dagger took and drove it deep
Into my heart.
   Balthasar. 'Twas not a proper knife.
   Romeo. Then we do live!
   Juliet. And living, we do love!
                     They embrace once more.
   Prince. This is a night of marvellous events;
Perhaps my kinsman Paris is not slain.   410
   Paris' Page. No, sire, he hath a herring's clammy look,
For he's filletted neatly as a cod,
'Pon some fishmonger's bench. His slimy guts—
   Prince. Enough! I think I have the picture of't.
   Romeo. I am the author of the fatal deed;
Pray let me take my bows beneath the axe.
   Montague. Nay, 'tis the fault of cursed Capulet
Whose matrimonial meddling doomed the Count.
   Capulet. I wished him wed, not dead, you whoreson knave!
   Montague. I am of pliant, supple whalebone made,   420
And you are glue; the insults that you hurl
Bounce off my buoyant frame and stick to you!
   Prince. O, cool thy heads, or I shall have them both!
But not yours, Romeo. Captain!
                 CAPTAIN *of the Watch advances*.
   Captain. Yes, my Lord!
   Prince. The Count's been murdered. Take with you some men
And round up those we usually suspect.
Do question them awhile on Paris' death,
Then free them.
           CAPTAIN *exits with some of Watch*.
Capulet and Montague,
You both had thought a son or daughter lost,
But each one of the other kind has gained,   430
And yet thou two doth squabble still. Shame, shame,
Come back, shame! These old men have need of you!
   Capulet. O brother Montague, I take all back!
   Montague. Dear Capulet, forgive me. Here's my hand.
                           They clasp hands.
   Capulet. Our childish feud, our too well-nourished grudge,
Is now our only issue that lies dead.
   Montague. And all that we shall bury here tonight
Are bitter hate and endless enmity.
            ROMEO, JULIET, CAPULET, &
               MONTAGUE *embrace*.
Prince. To these grave doings let us put an end.
Romeo, you are pardoned for your acts,   440
To others, too, my mercy shall extend.
Now go, and far and wide report these facts;
For lo, this story cannot have an equal,
Unless perchance someday there be a sequel!

THE EPILOGUE

                              Enter CHORUS.
Chorus. The moon-eyed pair, now rescued from the tomb,
Trades sigh for sigh, and kiss for honeyed kiss,
But Fate, who weaves our lives upon her loom,
In coming scenes will end this nuptial bliss.
Arrived in Venice on their wedding trip
The twain are set upon by persons vile
And placed in chains aboard a pirate ship
That bears them to a strange and secret isle.
In this far place, a fearsome monster dwells
Midst relics of some long-departed race.   10
There will be amulets and magic spells
And wizards for our newlyweds to face.
Miss not this triumph of the playwright's art:
Romeo and Juliet, the second part!

ARISTOTLE'S Aerobics

by the best-selling author of
Analytics, Ethics, Topics, Politics, Poetics, Physics,* and *Metaphysics

Because Aristotle's Aerobics *was transcribed and edited (323 B.C.) by his nephew and protegé Callisthenes, this practical shape-up dissertation has long (and erroneously) been known as the "Callisthenics." Although Aristotle's students idealized an "ethos" (or, as we might say, "lifestyle") of "wellness," young Athenians were by no means interested in maintaining a Spartan regime. The wily "Master of All-Natural Philosophy" therefore conducted his seminars in an easy-to-follow "Peripatetic" manner—while jogging.*

Although it's more than 2,000 years old, Aristotle's Aerobic Shape-Up Program is by no means out-of-date. And it's easy, too. In fact, you can start today in your own home—even if you don't have a personal trainer or, for that matter, an Attic tunic or a Doric column! (*Do* make sure you have the proper footwear, however. As the Master himself wrote in his *Nicomachean Ethics*: "It is impossible . . . to do noble acts without the proper equipment.")

Zeno's Paradox

Zeno of Elia, whom Aristotle called "the founder of dialectic," was the author of the famous paradox that bears his name. Simply put, it states that, in a foot race, even the fastest runner can never reach the finish line because, in an endless sequence of measurable periods of time, the racer will cover exactly half the distance to his goal, then half of the remaining distance, then half of *that* half, and so on. Whatever its merits as philosophy, Zeno's Paradox provided Aristotle with an ideal organizing principle for the popular "lifelong exercise program" he supervised at the Lyceum in Athens.

Step 1.

Find a nice, comfortable space for your workout. Position yourself two full strides from the nearest wall. Now, face that wall and step off powerfully toward it with your left foot. Be energetic, but don't overdo it. Keep in mind Aristotle's recommendation in Book I, Section 63, of *Diogenes Laertius*:

"Moderation in all things!"

Step 2.

Now, with your right foot, take another step, *precisely* half as long as your previous one. That was fun, wasn't it? You see, Aristotle was right when he wrote (in *Nicomachean Ethics*):

"Happiness . . . comes as a result of . . . training."

Step 3.

Using your left foot this time, repeat Step 2. Keep up the good work! Don't forget, as Aristotle tells us in his *Rhetorica ad Alexandrum,*

"One falls into ill health as the result of not caring for exercise."

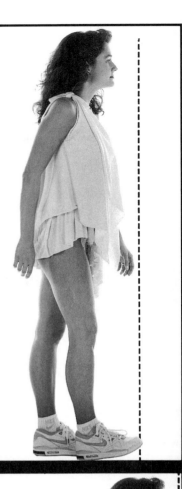

Step 4.

It's time for your right foot to get back into the act. Briskly but carefully position it so that your big toe is halfway between the big toe of your *left* foot and the base of the wall. A word of warning: It's at this point in the program that a lot of people drop out. It won't happen to you if you'll just keep in mind this helpful quotation from Aristotle's *Nicomachean Ethics*:

"Nothing is so pleasant or so lovable as . . . exercise."

Step 5,631,249.

It's your left foot's turn again. Move it half the distance to that wall! Hang in there and don't get discouraged! If you do, comfort yourself with the knowledge that, with every step, you're coming ever closer to meeting the almost impossibly strict standard for continuous movement spelled out in Section 6 of Aristotle's *Metaphysics:*

"There is no continuous movement except movement in place."

*GE may "bring good things to life," but sadly, it's a bit
too late for the troubled, brilliant poet Sylvia Plath.
She wasn't without a funnybone, however. The surprising
and delightful verses that follow, discovered stuffed inside
a recipe box shortly after her death, reveal a very different
gal than the tortured soul we thought we knew. Clearly, had
her stove been electric, we might have been blessed with
another Bombeck or Viorst!*

The Lighter Side of Sylvia Plath

Diet

My exercise instructor
is a Nazi ectomorph,
My "One Size Fits All" nylons
fit an anorexic dwarf,
Yes, Pillsbury sure said it best,
A chocolate cake says "lovin',"
The next time I see cottage cheese
My head goes in the oven!

Dinner Dishes

The children are helpful as mollusks,
My husband lies fetid as death,
I scream and I yell and I wheedle,
But why am I wasting my breath!?
Why not make my next inhalation
an eloquent statement with sass:
I'll leave them a sink full of dishes
And go stick my head in the gas!

I Love Life… It's *Living* I Can't Stand!

I love life,
It's *living* I can't stand!
I love weddings,
but who hired that damn band?!
I adore the seashore,
But not that bloody sand!
I love life . . .
It's *living* I can't stand!

I love writing,
but loathe this wretched chair!
I love my husband,
But hate his *guts,* so *there*!
I'd stick my head in the oven,
But I just washed my hair!
Yes, I love life . . .
It's *living* I can't bear!

*Aware of the vast profits to be reaped from the Am Lit 101 market,
a small concern determined to create its own textbook of
Great Poems, only to discover that most Great Poems, and quite
a few Not So Hot ones as well, had already been used up. Undeterred,
the plucky entrepreneurs renamed their company Ed Norton, Inc.,
and produced an original anthology, composed entirely of
sequels to better-known works.*

The Ed Norton Anthology of Underground Poetry Sequels

The Emperor of Frozen Yogurt

**Wallace Stevens wrote a lot of nice poems, no doubt, but
the only one we kind of remember is the one about the ice
cream. Only it wasn't really about ice cream, it was about
Death or Impermanence or something, and frankly when
we reread it it was looking a little tired, a tad frumpy, a
bit pre-war.** *The Ed Norton Anthology* **is proud to present
an update, a sort of Stevens Lite we know you'll find
refreshing.**

Call the curler of big freeweights,
The muscular dude, and bid him sell
In plastic cups cold tasteless curds.
Let the spokesmodels pose in such swimsuits
As they for SI wear, and let the boys
Bring seviche from this month's *Gourmet*.
Let condo be finale of yurt.
The only emperor is the emperor of frozen yogurt.

Take from the dresser of Memphis,
Lacking any recognizable knob, those jeans
On which she embroidered peace signs once
And rip them so as to cover her wealth.
If her fleshy hips protrude, they come
To show how old she is, and dumb.
Let Loni affix to Burt.
The only emperor is the emperor of frozen yogurt.

What I Scribe — Here in Amherst

by Emily Dickinson

No sooner have you forked over $39.95 for the latest, definitive *Collected Emily Dickinson* than some hyperacademic scavenger excavates another cache of cryptic stanzas stashed by the Belle of Amherst in some damn attic. The feminist poetry journal *Persephone* was stripped of its NEA funding after printing these verses in July 1990.

What I scribe—here in Amherst—
You cypher there—in class—
A spinster's conversation
Like whisperers, at Mass—

Apprentices conspiring—
As if we might grow wise—
Collecting—then dissecting—
A morning's Butterflies—

What unreceived Communion—
Mute—deaf—blind—Scholarship—
To wholly comprehend a tongue,
Who cannot read—a Lip—

The Word can be made Flesh—
The Key is in the Lock—
The Bee is in the Blossom—
The Bird is on the Walk—

The Train is in the Tunnel—
The Snake is in the Grass—
Put down this book—go out and get
Yourself a Piece of Ass—

The Road Taken

This surprisingly acrimonious sequel was discovered scribbled on the back of William Carlos Williams' invitation to the 1961 Presidential Inaugural festivities, during which Robert Frost received special recognition as the Kennedy Administration's "honored poet." It has never been finally determined who actually wrote "The Road Taken."

At a fork in the trail at the foot of a hill,
Where birches bend over a crumbling wall,
Just fooling around, the way boys will
Were Ezra and Tom and "Doctor" Bill,
And Robert, the cutest one of them all.

They bickered about which way to choose:
One path was scary and wild and steep,
They were none of them wearing sensible shoes;
Robert started to whine (and collapsed in a heap)
About miles to go, promises, needing his sleep . . .

One way, they knew, led back to town.
The other went straight up—who knows where?
And a long way up means a long way down,
A bad little boy might starve, or drown,
Alone and at risk, away up there . . .

But Ezra double-dared his peers:
"Old Walt would have done it the hard way, Tom!
Come on, 'Doc'! Let's be pioneers!"
So they left little Robert behind, in tears,
To take the known road back to Mom.

I suppose by now you've guessed this story
Is a fable of sorts—what the critics call
An extended trope, or an allegory:
Because Robert preferred repute to glory,
He made no difference at all.

A compact yet comprehensive introductory text that captures the entire majestic sweep of Western sequelization, brilliantly recounting the epic chronicle of a hundred centuries of human recreativity in less than a thousand words.

A Brief History of Art and Architecture Sequels

The Triumph of the Familiar

From that epochal moment ten thousand years ago when some unknown Cro-Magnon cave painter paused before his just completed drawing of a fleeing bison and then, rather than simply depicting additional animals encountered in the hunt, instead drew next to his original design a picture of the identical bison, wounded, and followed that image with a representation of the same bison lying dead, the history of art and the history of the sequel have been inextricably intertwined.

In fact, some of the oldest and purest statements of man's inexhaustible urge to produce sequels are also among the most enduring monuments of civilization: the pyramid of Cheops and its celebrated follow-ups, the pyramids of Chephren and Mycerinus; the Doric order of classical temples and its sequels, the Ionic and the Corinthian; and the cathedral of Notre-Dame and its sublime spin-offs,

DEAD BISON
Depictions of a dead bison from the multi-part wall painting known as the "Die Herd series" found in a cave at Lascaux in central France (and reproduced in Lascaux II, the sequel cave constructed by the French so the original cave could be sealed to protect its delicate decorated rock surfaces). These masterful animal studies—the earliest known sequel images—were created during the Ice Age, itself an update of the Stone Age and the prequel to the artistically important Bronze Age and Iron Age.

the cathedrals of Chartres, Reims, and Salisbury.

And the very Renaissance itself, as its name suggests, was in effect a great historical sequel—the deliberate continuation of the Greco-Roman golden age whose architectural and artistic traditions it so gloriously updated. Of course, the Renaissance also served as the essential prequel to the culturally important Reformation, which in turn sparked its own historic remake, the Counter-Reformation, which led directly to the Baroque and its inevitable follow-up, the Rococo, which preceded the two great stylistic revivals, Neo-Classicism and Neo-Gothic Romanticism, which set the stage for Impressionism and its immediate sequel, Post-Impressionism.

Throughout all of these periods, in addition to playing important roles in the great consequential historical movements of which they were a part, individual artists also produced indisputable mastersequels on their own. Among these major "reworks of art" probably the best known ones—other than those we have chosen to illustrate—are Goya's *Naked Maja* and its follow-up, *The Clothed Maja;* Monet's long and enormously popular series of water lily paintings; and Andrew Wyeth's cycle of "Helga" paintings (alas, there is not room to reproduce these particular examples here, but they will appear in the sequel to this essay, "A Slightly Longer History of Art and Architecture Sequels").

But the final triumph of the art sequel had to await the appearance of nonrepresentational art and "modern" architecture in the postwar period. This dramatic development led to the creation of a veritable cornucopia of abstract remasterpieces, among the most notable of which are Jackson Pol-

THE VISITOR ORIENTATION CENTER AT THE GREAT PYRAMID AT GIZA

One now finds it hard to recall the Louvre without I. M. Pei's Visitor Orientation Center, so strikingly does the stark postmodernism of the addition stand in contrast to the flowing lines of the grand *musée*. The success of the building made it clear that a good pyramid fits right in anywhere, and the architectural firm of I. M. Too designed this center at Giza in hopes of achieving the same dramatic interplay between old and new.

THE WORLD TRADE CENTER AT PISA, OR THE "LEANING TWIN TOWERS"

The audacious simplicity of Minoru Yamasaki's design for the World Trade Center in New York City left many architects grumbling "Why didn't *I* think of that?" This stunning annex to Italy's most famous monument to poor engineering demonstrates the same refreshing whimsy. Tourism revenues in the little town have doubled, and the popular rooftop cafe *Windows On Pisa* offers a view of the ground below that's truly a treat for the inner ear.

lock's paintings of swirling dribbles, brilliantly continued in his paintings of dribbling swirls; Mark Rothko's brooding blotches of purple and brown, followed so naturally by his brooding blotches of blue, black, and red; and Jasper Johns' flags, and their simple but powerful sequels, more flags, and still more flags (sadly, once again we lack the room to include works by these artists, even though our space limitations are nowhere nearly as severe as those in our prequel, "An Even Briefer History of Art and Architecture Sequels"). And this same modernist movement produced the single strongest statement of the dominance of creative continuity in contemporary culture: the International Style of architecture epitomized by New York's Seagram building and Lever House and their 11,787 sequels in cities around the world.

What does the future hold? In a word, the past, for even the most cursory study of art history reveals one fundamental reality: Creation and repetition are but two sides of the same coin, and since it is that coin, after all, that the artist seeks, he or she must always remember that people may not know much about art, but they know what they like, and what they like, they'd like some more of.

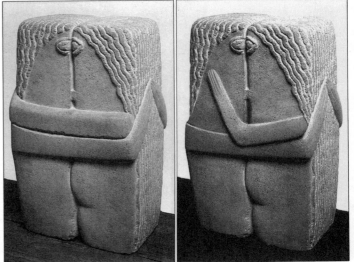

THE SLAP

Constantin Brancusi's *The Kiss* (1908) was followed by the powerful *The Slap* (1909, pictured at right), the second of a three-part series. The third, entitled *Date Rape* (1910), was termed indecent and banned from exhibition at the Salon des Indépendants. Brancusi was far ahead of his time, both as a forerunner of the Cubist movement in sculpture and in his pioneering commitment to bringing a very serious and underreported crime to light.

GENESIS II

This exquisite page from a recently unearthed fifteenth-century Florentine illuminated manuscript sets the imagination whirling with its implications. Do we dare believe the strong evidence suggesting that it may indeed be the work of Michelangelo? If proven authentic, this profoundly important discovery will have immeasurable impact on both the art world and Western religion. Sequels to the Word of God are not without precedent (The New Testament; Paul's Chain Letter to the Corinthians, reprinted elsewhere in this book), but *Genesis II* will surely stand as the "re-Creation" of all time.

Genesis II

On the eighth day God woke up.

THE EATEN GYPSY (above)

Henri Rousseau's famous *The Sleeping Gypsy* (1897), which was believed to have initially been entitled *The Regurgitated Gypsy,* seems in fact to have been the sequel to the recently discovered *The Eaten Gypsy* (1896). As the painter evolved beyond his roots as a Primitive, perhaps he considered the original title of his better-known masterpiece tasteless. Whether prequel or sequel, *The Eaten Gypsy* lays to rest the notion that Rousseau had no sense of humor.

THE DIVORCE OF THE ARNOLFINIS (opposite page)

The tabloids had a field day with the breakup of the Arnolfinis, one of the more visible fun couples of ultra-rich fifteenth-century Flemish society. So messy was the split, and so tempting the offer from *Volk* magazine for a painting to reproduce in its May 1435 issue, that artist Jan Van Eyck, who just a year earlier had completed the official *wedding* portrait of Giovanni Arnolfini and his bride, was inspired once again to capture the couple in oil.

NUDE REASCENDING A STAIRCASE (left)

Color transparencies of Marcel Duchamp's little-known rendering of a climbing nude are frequently reproduced upside down and mistakenly identified as *Nude Descending a Staircase,* an earlier and, in the opinion of the American Sequel Society, inferior Duchamp painting. Our researchers continue in their efforts to locate the original work.

Moby-Dick II: Raise the Pequod!

An incredible discovery made by a descendant of the sole survivor of Captain Ahab's fatal voyage leads Commander Dipp Schmidt into a desperate contest with his ruthless nemesis, KGB Colonel Viktor Tiktov, to find a long-lost secret that could change the world—or end it!

The Pentagon—May 15

"Don't call me, Ishmael—I'll call you," Admiral Charles "Chuck" Chairweather barked into the telephone. The short, stocky Chief of Naval Operations slammed the handset into its cradle and stabbed the intercom button.

"If that pipsqueak calls again, don't put him through," the nation's second highest-ranking naval officer rasped into the aptly named "squawk box." At the other end, Petty Officer Doris Chestly struggled to control her heavy breathing as she said "Aye-aye, sir," then slipped back under her desk where Commander Dipp Schmidt was taking her, hard and fast.

"How was I?" the busty, curvaceous secretary breathed when she was once more seated at her typewriter.

The rugged, 40-year old former Navy SEAL commando eyed her appraisingly as he straightened the knot of his tie under his sharply chiseled, almost hazardous chin. "Like an aerobic cheetah in a prop trunk," he said.

The intercom buzzed again. "As soon as Commander Schmidt comes, send him in."

Petty Officer Chestly's full, sensuous lips broke into a wide grin. "Commander Schmidt just came, sir," she said briskly into the squat, black communications device.

Dipp winked at her with one of his cold, gray eyes and then blew her a kiss that neatly snapped off both of her earrings. Chestly was startled until she remembered from Schmidt's file that in addition to speaking Russian and seven other languages fluently and possessing a photographic memory, the much-decorated expert on undersea warfare was a master of a number of Oriental martial arts, including Kong Flu, an obscure Chinese fighting method whose practitioners can break a man's neck from 40 feet away with a single, well-placed sneeze. She shuddered involuntarily. She had seen Dipp's warm side; she never wanted to see the cold side that she knew lay hidden beneath the surface, brutally defying the elementary rules of heat transfer between adjacent layers.

"How was I?" the busty, curvaceous secretary breathed.

2

TIME OUT!
Isis Satori-Bernstein,
a psychic and herbal-
wrap therapist from
Santa Barbara, Cali-
fornia, wrote us to
describe a remark-
able experience. It
seems she was chan-
neling the Emperor
Cheops for the dis-
traught victim of a
botched liposuction,
when the ancient
Egyptian ruler sud-
denly seized the
moment to air a gripe
of his own. "He really
shared," Isis
recounts. "He said he
was incredibly disap-
pointed with the
Afterlife. He was sort
of whiny. Like how
there was nothing to
do, and how he got
lousy send-off
presents... And he
especially hated *The
Egyptian Book of
the Dead*. He said
everybody in the
Afterlife hates it. It
bores them to tears.
And then he told me
this great idea..."

Well, Isis, in the bot-
tom corner of the
following left-hand
pages, you and the
Emperor will find a
work that breathes
new life into that
dusty old downer:

THE EGYPTIAN FLIP BOOK OF THE DEAD

"Welcome aboard, Schmidt," said the Admiral, whose use of salty sea terms, Dipp knew, was a transparent attempt by the paper-pushing military bureaucrat to hide the fact that the only water he had seen in the last 20 years was the Potomac River. "What's the poop on that new Russkie pigboat?"

Dipp dropped a bulky report on the Admiral's immaculate desk. "It's all here, sir, and worse than we feared," he said gravely. "Their experimental Bravo-class missile sub is, despite its NATO designation, nothing to cheer about. It's so quiet, we can't detect it. It's as silent as death—and just as deadly."

"Dammit, Dipp, glasnost or no glasnost, a sub like that is a shot across our bows. If the Soviets can slip through our sonobuoy arrays in the Greenland–Iceland–United Kingdom gap, they can station those babies right off the Virginia coast and lob cruise missiles at our key command centers before we know what hit us right between the eyes like a ton of winged bricks."

"Yes, Admiral," said Dipp solemnly, though inwardly he smiled at the CNO's obvious concern for the vulnerability of his own headquarters. "Gorbachev may be playing us for the biggest patsies since the Greeks pulled that Trojan Horse trick—only this time, the treacherous steed will be carrying 500 megatons of nuclear destruction, and it will be virtually undetectable under 600 feet of water."

"Yes," agreed the Admiral, "and by contrast, it won't be some Bronze Age city in Asia Minor that gets wiped off the map—it will be Washington, D.C. There are probably some other differences," the Admiral added grimly, "but they pale by comparison to the ones we've already identified."

"By the way, Admiral, just to digress for a moment," said Dipp, changing the subject with the unexpected, lightning-fast turn of phrase that lets initiates into the ancient Laotian art of Lop Chat dominate any conversation totally by using a single powerful "Tiger Clause," "I couldn't help overhearing your instructions to Miss Chestly about Ishmael. Is that by any chance the Ishmael of the Woods Hole Oceanographic Institute, who is the world's leading expert on communication with marine mammals and the great-great-great-grandson of the Ishmael who sailed on the *Pequod* with Captain Ahab?"

"Yes, that's him," admitted Admiral Chairweather. "That harebrained whipper-snapper keeps calling with a boatload of poppycock about how he can communicate with whales and wouldn't the Navy like to chip in a few million bucks for his research." The Admiral rapped his desk for emphasis. "All I need is for a bunch of wooly-headed environmentalists and left-leaning journalists to find out we've bankrolled a language lab for Fudgie the Whale and his finny friends, and I'll be the whipping-boy for the animal-rights lobby, not to mention the laughingstock of the congressional arms committees."

Dipp winced at this eloquent expression of the Cover Your Ass mentality that had undoubtedly done more damage to the Navy than the whole Walker family of spies, including their little-known, but amazingly devious dog, Mutzie.

"Let me follow it up, Admiral," Dipp suggested. "I'll concede it's a long shot—hell, it would be like winning a game of Monopoly with one house each on Baltic and Mediterranean, the Waterworks, and a single railroad, but if it pans out, we may have found the way to end all ways of attacking this new Russian sub."

"And if it doesn't work?" Chairweather countered.

"Then you throw away the memo you're going to write strongly urging me to proceed with the project and keep the other memo you're also going to write warning me that it's a total waste of time and money," said Dipp with a sly look.

Admiral Chairweather started to protest, but just shook his head and laughed. "You're insubordinate, Dipp, but you have a way of getting results," he said, his voice betraying his grudging respect for the independent-minded, authority-defying Schmidt whose legendary exploits as a top operative of the supersecret, black-budget Defense Projects Board had won the admiration of the handful of top government officials who held a security clearance high enough to hear about them.

"Miss Chestly, give Commander Schmidt Ishmael's phone number on his way out," said Chairweather into the intercom.

And yours, too, thought Dipp, wondering how the surprisingly athletic Petty Officer would perform when released from the confines of her desk and the regulation naval uniform that contained but did not conceal the ample curves of her shapely figure.

3

Schmidt went directly from the Admiral's office to the Washington Metro stop below the Pentagon's gloomy shopping mall. One of the sleek Blue Line trains headed for National Airport whispered into the station as he reached the platform and 20 minutes later he was seated in the nearly deserted rearmost section of a Boston-bound shuttle taxiing toward the end of the runway. He punched Ishmael's telephone number into an Airfone with one hand while with the other he caressed the high, longing breasts of the young, red-headed cabin attendant who had taken the seat next to him.

"*Commander* Schmidt?" Ishmael inquired hopefully when he came on the line. "You must be from Admiral Chairweather's office."

"Let's just say that the Admiral told me you have a *whale* of an idea, and I've decided to fly up from Washington to talk to you about it. I should be at your lab"—Dipp did a rapid calculation—"by 5 o'clock this afternoon. O.K.?"

"Thank God you called," exclaimed the excited voice on the other end of the line. "I've made a revolutionary discovery! The fate of the free world may hang in the balance. If I'm right, we can—"

Dipp cut him off in midsentence. "Hold it, Ishmael! This is not a secure line! We'll talk when I get there." He abruptly broke the connection.

"For your comfort and convenience, I do ask that you be in a full upright position during all takeoffs and landings," begged the cabin attendant as she lowered herself onto Dipp's firm, almost cruel lap.

The three high-bypass turbofans of the 727 came to life in a sudden surging rush of power that was perfectly synchronized with another powerful thrusting as both the plane and the two occupants of seat 42-D reached the point of no return simultaneously.

M.S. **Red Tide,** *Lat. 41°13′ N., Long. 72°38′ W.—May 15*

Captain Ivan Churkov watched with amused detachment as the deck crew winched in a net half full of glistening, silvery fish, and then, as the American Coast Guard plane disappeared over the horizon, released the startled sea creatures, who turned the waters by the ship's rust-streaked sides into a boiling, sudsy foam in their eagerness to escape.

The charade of setting out and winding in the huge drag nets was a monotonous yet necessary part of maintaining the outward appearance of a law-abiding oceangoing trawler, but it had nothing whatsoever to do with the *Red Tide*'s real purpose. She was a fish-

The cabin attendant lowered herself onto Dipp's firm, almost cruel lap . . .

ing vessel all right, but she did her fishing in the invisible electromagnetic waves above the ship, not those in which she rolled and pitched on this bright, cold spring day in the Atlantic off Long Island.

Satisfied with the realistic-looking activity abovedecks, Churkov descended the main companionway and entered the immense radio room that was the center of the ship and the whole reason for her existence. The walls were lined with a bewildering array of long- and short-wave radio receivers and transmitters, microwave detectors, tape recorders, decoding and encryption machinery, and countless other devices whose arcane functions Churkov only vaguely understood, all lit with the flickering light of oscilloscopes, radar displays, and computer video screens. Nearly 40 technicians sat or stood at these instruments, listening intently to earphones, adjusting dials, monitoring displays, and flicking switches.

As he entered, a printer began clacking, and Radio Operator Third Class Igor Souchev immediately went over to it, and as soon as it stopped, he tore off the page, read it quickly, then excitedly handed it to Captain Churkov.

"Sir, our key-phrase microwave scanner has intercepted a telephone call from Washington National Airport to the Woods Hole Oceanographic Institute with three trigger-word groups!" he reported.

Churkov examined the message that the ship's ultrasensitive receiving equipment had snatched from the air. Its importance was unmistakable: "revolutionary discovery," "fate of the free world," and "hangs in the balance" were at the top of the list of five critical terms the *Red Tide* was always listening for. The only ones missing from the incredible intercept were "alter the future course of history" and "change forever the world as we know it."

"Well done, Souchev," said the Captain. "Transmit this transcript immediately by direct satellite burst to Murmansk Central, Priority Level Omega-One."

He pulled her mouth to his and kissed her so hard she moaned.

While he waited for the response from Naval Intelligence Headquarters, Churkov shook his head in wonder at the extraordinary gullibility of the Americans, who, dazzled by glasnost, had sold their most advanced computers to the Soviet Ministry of Agriculture to use for crop forecasts. Now, completely reprogrammed and mated to the antennas bought from the English, the amplifiers obtained from the Germans, and the digital tape recorders purchased from the Japanese, the microprocessors could perform the unbelievably complex task of plucking a single word out of 10 million telephone calls, which in security-lax America almost always contained an open-air microwave relay for some part of the circuit.

The speed of the reply from the top-secret installation on the Kola Peninsula underscored the importance of the intercept. Churkov took the brief directive to his cabin, personally decoded it, then dialed the combination to his safe. He opened an envelope, extracted a card, and carried it back to the radio room.

"I have a job for you, Souchev," he said, handing the oblong piece of paper to the radioman, who briefly examined it, then went to his console, put on his combination earphone-microphone headset, and punched some numbers into a keypad.

One hundred fifteen nautical miles away, a telephone began to ring in an apartment in a small town on Cape Cod. After three and a half rings, an answering machine came on, and Souchev, who like all the members of his Surveillance Team spoke fluent, unaccented English, left a short, innocent-sounding message.

He leaned back in his chair and smiled in satisfaction. This truly was a memorable day. Yes, he had made important intercepts in the past, but he had never before participated in the activation of a KGB deep-cover sleeper agent.

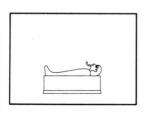

Woods Hole—May 15

Schmidt nosed the rental car into a space in the visitors' parking lot of the Oceanographic Institute and strode inside. A slender, boyishly handsome young man with a shock of sandy hair was pacing nervously in the reception area. As soon as Dipp gave his name to the well-endowed blonde who sat at the switchboard, he stepped forward, thrust out his hand and said, "Gee, I'm glad to see you, Commander Schmidt. I'm Ishmael, and what I have to show you could alter the future course of history and change forever the world as we know it!"

"Call me Dipp," said Schmidt, grimacing at the scientist's unguarded optimism.

Ishmael looked at his watch. It was 5:30. "Boy, we've got to get a move on," he said. "We need to be at the harbor by six at the latest."

Dipp looked at the receptionist. She slowly moved her tongue over her soft, red lips. He shrugged his shoulders. "Business before pleasure," he said, then pulled her mouth to his and kissed her so hard she moaned.

2

They drove the short distance to the old whaling port's harbor in Ishmael's battered jeep. "Is this your first time on the Cape?" Ishmael inquired politely.

"Nope," said Dipp. "I was here a few years back when Abu Kabal and a team of Libyan terrorists slipped ashore from a submarine, attacked the Kennedy compound in Hyannisport, and held the Senator and six other members of the family hostage."

"I never heard about that!" Ishmael exclaimed.

"Yeah," said Dipp bitterly, "we never get to talk about the ones we win."

Ishmael parked the car at the Martha's Vineyard ferry landing and led Dipp out to the end of a long, rickety-looking pier where a lone figure dressed in blue jeans and a parka stood looking out toward the harbor mouth.

"Stacey, he's here," Ishmael called out excitedly.

Stacey Romano turned around, and Dipp involuntarily caught his breath. She was gorgeous. She had the silken mystery of Garbo, the smoky allure of Lauren Bacall, and the torrid torso of Brigitte Bardot.

She gave Ishmael a quick kiss on his cheek, then turned to Dipp, who, struck by something oddly aristocratic about her bearing, startled her by kissing her hand. "Commander Dipp Schmidt, at your service," he said with a self-mocking grin.

"This is Stacey Romano," said Ishmael proudly. "She works at the Marine Biological Lab. Are you ready, honey?"

"Y-yes, I g-guess so," Stacey stammered. "Here goes nothing," she smiled nervously, and turning to face the waters of Nantucket Sound, she produced a series of eerie high-pitched warbles that were part hum, part whistle, and part singsong birdcalls.

"Stacey is the only person we've ever encountered who can make sounds in the ultrasonic registers that whales use for long-distance communication—sounds beyond the range of the average person's hearing," Ishmael explained. "There's a small group of whales that's been just offshore at this time of day for the last two weeks—Stacey is going to try to get them to spout for us on command."

Suddenly, a half-dozen large, gray forms surfaced in a tight group less than 100 yards from the end of the pier.

With a sharp sighing sound, the huge creatures emitted thick jets of vaporized water

She had the mystery of Garbo, the allure of Lauren Bacall, and the torso of Brigitte Bardot . . .

in perfect unison, and then, after pausing momentarily as if waiting for further instructions, they swam slowly away, the powerful flukes of their massive, triangular tails churning the murky waters of the narrow harbor.

"My God," said Dipp as the bulky marine mammals disappeared from view, "if we can communicate with the whales, we may be able to convince them to throw their considerable weight behind the navies of the free world, and if they were to do so, these hefty babies could shift the balance of sea power decisively in our favor once and for all!"

"War," Stacey hissed. "That's all you men ever think of! Haven't the whales had enough of slaughter and bloodshed? Must we use the gift of language in a cynical effort to turn these noble animals into mere foot soldiers, albeit large ones, in our endless geopolitical maneuverings?" She stormed off down the pier.

"Stacey, wait!" Ishmael shouted and turned to follow her.

"No, Ishmael, let her go," said Dipp, putting a hand on his elbow in the classic "Inhibit the Passionate Dragon" hold of Noh Khanh Doo, the Korean art of arm-twisting. If he had wanted, by adding a simple thumb jab Dipp could have persuaded Ishmael to withdraw from a race for elective office at the prefecture level or to forgo opening a restaurant devoted solely to noodle dishes.

"She's got to let off a little steam," Dipp continued, thinking of how nice it would be to have his hands on her valves during that process.

"She—she gets so emotional about the whales," said Ishmael.

Dipp scowled. Why was it every time things were going smoothly some screwy dame with a head full of pacifist hooey had to come along to throw a gorilla-sized monkey wrench smack-dab into the middle of the works?

"What if she gets it in her pretty little head that we're bad news for her ponderous pals and she tells them 'Back away! Leave! Dive! Flee!'?" asked Dipp.

Ishmael thought for a moment and then smiled ruefully. "The good news is, for the foreseeable future I can absolutely guarantee that those words will never pass Stacey's lips in whale language. Unfortunately, that's also the bad news."

A frown creased Dipp's deeply etched brow, wrinkling the small patch of scar tissue where a 9mm bullet had creased his scalp during a somewhat heated exchange of views with the KGB in Gorky Park in Moscow over who would take custody of an obscure railway official who also happened to be Grand Duke Nicholas, the last man alive with a legal claim to the throne of Imperial Russia.

"What's the problem?" Dipp grunted. "Your demonstration made whale communication look as easy as A-B-C."

Ishmael nodded glumly. "It *is* as easy as A-B-C, and *that's* the problem. Look, Dipp, my house is just a couple of blocks from here. I have something there that will explain everything—something incredible."

3

Ishmael opened the door to a small, gray-shingled colonial house that faced Woods Hole's tiny, boat-crammed harbor. Inside, it looked exactly as it probably had in 1850, with low ceilings, a huge brick fireplace, simple handcrafted furniture, a few childish-looking American primitive paintings on the walls, and bits of nautical gear—a chronometer, a sextant, even a harpoon blade—displayed on shelves and tables. In the center of the room, placed incongruously on a long, low table, was a dark wooden coffin intricately carved with strange, curving designs.

> *"War," Stacey hissed. "That's all you men ever think of!"*

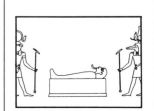

"My God," Dipp gasped, "Those markings! They can only mean one thing—this must be Queequeg's coffin!"

"How did you know?" Ishmael exclaimed in astonishment.

"I did my Ph.D. thesis at Annapolis on the evolution of hull design from Cleopatra's barge to the Hobie Cat. *Moby-Dick* was an important part of my researches into the development of the keelson. So, it *was* a true story."

"Yes," said Ishmael emphatically. "And this is the very same coffin on which my great-great-great-grandfather, the original Ishmael, floated safely away from the wreck of the *Pequod*. I found it hidden behind a false wall when I was restoring this house. I inherited it from my father—the fourth Ishmael—when he died last year."

"I like what you've done with the floors," said Dipp. "Low-gloss polyurethane?"

"Yeah, two coats. Tough as nails, but none of that plasticky shine."

"Then the first Ishmael lived here after he came back on the *Rachel*?"

"That's right," said Ishmael. "In those days, Woods Hole was a whaling port, and although my ancestor never went to sea again, he liked to live among whalemen. And it was in this same house that Herman Melville interviewed him for *Moby-Dick*."

"Other than to name the chief character in the story after him, Melville never gave credit to your forebear in the book," Dipp remarked. "I wonder why."

Ishmael opened a desk drawer and removed a stack of small, thin notebooks. "It's all spelled out here in these notebooks that he filled with his reminiscences of the doomed voyage. I found them in the coffin. It seems that Melville wanted to give a proper acknowledgment to Ishmael, but Ishmael wouldn't let him—he was angry because Melville refused to tell the whole story."

"Good Lord," said Dipp, "*Moby-Dick* is the literary equivalent of a garage sale! I can't believe Melville omitted anything even remotely related to whaling—why, he even included a recipe for cooking whales' brains!"

"And yet, he did leave something out—something of the utmost importance," said Ishmael animatedly. "The original Ishmael was convinced that Captain Ahab's uncanny skill at locating whales was based on his ability to understand and to speak the whale language, and he reconstructed from memory the details of several specific occasions on which he saw and heard the mad old man communicating with whales. Listen to this." He opened one of the notebooks at a marked page and began to read:

> On the night before that ill-omened day when we for the first time encountered Moby-Dick and began the chase that ended with the loss of the *Pequod* and all her crew save only myself alone, I happened to come on deck in the middle of the last watch, my slumbers having been disturbed by a peculiar singing sound so faint that only one as keen of hearing as I am could ever hearken to it, and so unearthly that when I first heard it, I thought I was still in the midst of some uneasy dream. There I espied Captain Ahab seated upon his ivory stool, his peg leg resting on the taffrail, the whalebone gleaming whitely in the bright moonlight. I crept silently closer and crouching in the shadow of the try-works, I watched in completest astonishment as Ahab peered in intense concentration at his alabaster limb as if reading something inscribed thereon, following which he cupped his hands around his mouth to amplify the sound and proceeded to emit that very same eerie musical wail which had awakened me. Almost at once, I heard the sound of a whale in the waters alongside the ship and the hiss of a spout, and then for nearly a quarter of an hour I witnessed the strangest colloquy that any man can ever have beheld as the wild-eyed captain and the great fish exchanged who knows what challenges and insults until at last, with one final slap of its flukes, the whale swam away.

"That's incredible," said Dipp. "And that's probably why Melville wouldn't use it in the book—he just didn't believe it."

"Or he did believe it, but he reckoned that no one else would," suggested Ishmael,

"I like what you've done with the floors," said Dipp.

"and he feared that an account of an actual conversation with a whale would have fatally undermined the credibility of an already fantastic tale."

"Did Ishmael have the key to Ahab's code?"

"No. I went over every page of his notebooks, every word he ever wrote. Nothing. But then I remembered from Chapter 108 of *Moby-Dick* that at the same time that the ship's carpenter was making Queequeg's coffin, he also made a new whalebone leg for Ahab, whose old leg had shattered when he was getting into a whaleboat. It occurred to me that by some crazy chance, the carpenter might just have used a leftover piece of the leg for the coffin frame. After all, lightweight, durable whalebone was a highly prized shipboard construction material."

Dipp whistled. "Talk about long shots! That makes winning the lottery look as easy as getting a ticket for parking a Rolls-Royce with out-of-state plates in front of a fire hydrant on Fifth Avenue on the day before Christmas during a snow emergency after giving a cop on the sidewalk a dime because you mistook him for a Salvation Army fund-raiser!"

"Yes, it was a billion-to-one shot," Ishmael agreed, "but I got lucky!"

He lifted the tightly fitting lid of the strangely carved coffin, exposing the smooth planks of the interior whose seams were still sealed with the caulking that had transformed the box into a life buoy. Attached to the wide slabs of wood were five crosspieces, one of which was a yellowish-white color. Ishmael took it out and handed it to Dipp.

"Whalebone!" Dipp whistled.

"Yes!" Ishmael confirmed, "and look at what's carved on it!"

On its upper surface, the strip of ivory-hued material was plain, but on its reverse side, a row of letters and a series of corresponding musical notes had been deeply incised into the polished fragment.

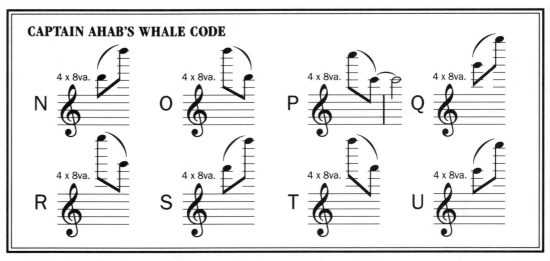

CAPTAIN AHAB'S WHALE CODE

"It can't be!" Dipp exclaimed.

"But it *is*," said Ishmael. "It's a piece of Ahab's broken peg leg with eight letters of the whale alphabet."

"By God, it's the Rosetta Bone!" Dipp declared.

"Only part of it, I'm afraid. We managed to compose the word 'spout' from the letters we had, and Stacey and I tested it out. You saw the results yourself. It works. The whales understand it."

"We must have the rest of that code!" said Dipp, slamming a gnarled fist into a weathered palm. "Our country's very survival may depend on it!"

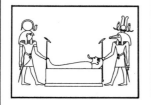

Ishmael looked disconsolate. ''I dismantled the coffin piece by piece, and there is no more whalebone in it. I ran what we had through our supercomputers at the Institute to see if any of the missing letters could be generated from some hidden underlying language pattern. No such pattern exists. The only way we will ever get the rest of the alphabet is to find the remaining pieces of Ahab's leg, and if they still exist at all, they're on the *Pequod,* which sank in the central Pacific 150 years ago.''

''Then we have only one choice,'' said Dipp gravely.

''You don't mean . . .?'' Ishmael gasped.

''I do.''

''But surely you can't be serious!''

''I am.''

''You actually plan to—''

''We must—''

''Raise the *Pequod*!'' they both cried simultaneously, Ishmael with disbelief, Dipp with that mixture of defiance and sheer bravado that gained him the instant respect of men and the passionate surrender of women. Women like the well-endowed receptionist from the Oceanographic Institute who, later that night in Dipp's room at the Spouter Inn and Motor Court, also spoke of a whalebone, but with moans of awe and ecstasy.

The well-endowed receptionist also spoke of a whalebone, but with awe and ecstasy.

THE LAST VOYAGE OF THE PEQUOD

Petropavlovsk · Aleutian Islands · Beijing · Japan · Hong Kong · Taiwan · Philippines · Guam · Borneo · Java · Australia · INTERNATIONAL DATE LINE · TROPIC OF CANCER · Los Angeles · Hawaiian Islands · Palmyra Island · Fanning Island · EQUATOR

Path of the *Pequod*

The White House—May 16

The President tossed the report onto the heavy oak desk that had been made from timbers taken from Nelson's flagship, the *Ark-Royal,* and presented to one of his predecessors by Queen Victoria. He walked over to the large, turn-of-the-century globe that stood against a curved wall in the Oval Office and spun it until the Pacific Ocean came into view. He pointed at the wide swath of faded blue sea he had exposed and turned to address Dipp.

"Commander Schmidt, if I remember my high school geography, the Pacific has an area of 70 million square miles—a little less than one third of the entire earth's surface. It's a vast expanse of salt water into which *twenty* countries the size of the United States could fit comfortably. Now, assuming I approve this cockamamie scheme of yours, how in H-E-double-hockeysticks are you going to find the wreck of one tiny wooden ship in all that salinated H_2O, let alone raise it?"

Dipp strode over to the globe and put a sinewy forefinger on a spot not far from the Equator. "Mr. President, we know from the ship's log of the *Rachel,* the whaling vessel that rescued the original Ishmael, that he was found at latitude 6°05′ North, longitude 162°11′ West. And we know from *Moby-Dick* that the *Pequod* was heading southeast toward Fanning Island and had just passed some seal rocks when she had the final, fatal encounter with the white whale. Those seal rocks are almost certainly part of Kingman Reef, and allowing for currents and prevailing wind conditions at the time of the year she sank, we've narrowed the position of the wreck of the *Pequod* to about ten square kilometers of mostly shallow water north of Palmyra Island, a U.S. possession 1,100 miles due south of Hawaii."

The President snorted derisively. "That's still like finding a needle in a haystack, but a haystack that contains the total annual hay production of the European Community, which, if I remember my most recent Economic Assessment Briefing correctly, is 44 million metric tons."

"And that needle isn't even made out of steel," observed General Cole Slaughton, the President's brilliant, but ruthless, National Security Adviser, "so you won't be able to use metal detection equipment, will you, Commander?"

Dipp let a small smile play across his grim lips. "On the contrary, General. You see, although the *Pequod* was constructed of wood, like all whaling ships she carried a pair of huge, 250-gallon iron try-pots for rendering whale blubber into oil, which were mounted over twin furnaces with heavy iron doors and sides. If we get within 1,000 meters of that baby, the metal detectors are going to light up like a Vegas slot machine that just hit a million-dollar jackpot!"

The President walked over to the thick bulletproof windows that faced the Washington monument, then turned and faced Dipp. "Do you have any idea what you're asking me to do?" he said. "In a time of mounting budget deficits and painful spending cutbacks, you're suggesting that we spend God knows how many millions of dollars to search for and then raise a long-lost whaling ship that may—just may—contain somewhere in its rotten, battered hulk a couple of scraps of whalebone only a few inches wide and less than a foot in length?"

"That about sums it up, sir," Dipp confirmed.

"And if we come up empty-handed, and there's a leak somewhere, and the fertilizer hits the windmill, some hotshot politician with an ax to grind could rake us over the coals to feather his own nest and leave us hanging out to dry without a leg to stand on, regardless of whether anyone's ox was gored! My God, it would make the Iran-Contra affair look like the Cherry Blossom Festival!"

"It would be Salt-Watergate," agreed Slaughton. "Mr. President, can we afford to take this risk?"

"Considering the Russkies' new Bravo-class missile boats, can we afford *not* to, sir?" said Dipp. "The whales have the potential of being the best damn antisubmarine warriors the world has ever known. Do we want to take the chance that some Soviet scientist

Dipp let a smile play across his grim lips.

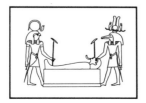

will stumble on the secret of whale communication and fill these as yet unaligned leviathans' massive heads with a bunch of brotherhood-of-mammals bushwah that will brainwash them into becoming misguided but willing minions of Moscow in its age-old plan to turn this planet into a totalitarian hellhole?''

"Now that you put it that way, Dipp, I see no choice but to proceed!" said the President, slapping his desk in emphasis. "I'm authorizing the Cetus Project!"

"You won't regret this, sir," said Dipp firmly.

"That's what you said when you came up with that half-baked scheme to arrest the Ayatollah in Teheran and bring him to America for trial," snapped General Slaughton.

"That was bad luck, not bad planning," Dipp shot back. "How the hell could we know the old buzzard would croak the moment we slapped the cuffs on him?"

The Kremlin—May 16

The President of the Soviet Union let the report drop on his heavy oak desk. It was an exact copy of the desk used by the President of the United States, painstakingly duplicated down to the last detail by Ministry of Works craftsmen from plans stolen from the British Museum.

"Comrade Chairman, I have read your report and your recommendations. I agree with your assessment of the threat—if what your agent has discovered is accurate, the Americans have indeed stumbled on the perfect way to foil our new experimental Bravo-class submarine, the *Prolonged Stormy Applause*. But the plan you propose would cost us millions of rubles we can ill afford and require us to reveal prematurely one of our most carefully guarded military secrets."

"Comrade President, we cannot allow the Americans to possess the secret of communicating with the whales," said the Chairman of the KGB. "Not only will it permit them to counter the most effective weapon we have ever devised, but it will also enable them to increase immeasurably their already overwhelming domination of the seas."

The President's Chief Adviser on Matters Affecting the Security of the Motherland, who had sat silently through the discussion, now spoke up. "Although I concur that the situation is grave, I would be remiss, Comrade President, if I did not emphasize the high stakes involved. While we need not concern ourselves with finding the *Pequod*—the Americans will perform that tiresome chore for us—if we attempt to seize or destroy it, we will certainly provoke a confrontation that will at the very least eradicate several years of your patient efforts to convince the West of our good intentions and at the worst trigger World War III."

"Yes," agreed the President. "It would make the downing of the Korean Air Liner look like the Festival of the Cabbage Blossoms."

"It could precipitate a naval Chernobyl," the Chief Adviser warned. "Can we afford to take the risk?"

The KGB Chairman shot the Chief Adviser a glance of pure loathing. "Comrade President, can we afford *not* to? The whales could provide us with an incredibly effective method of locating the American ballistic missile fleet, whose total invulnerability is the only factor standing between us and an absolute first-strike capability. And do we wish to sit idly by while the capitalists use their slick advertising techniques to poison the minds of these mighty but unenlightened laborers of the deep with cynical pie-in-the-sky materialistic promises that will turn them into unwitting dupes of Washington in its never-ending plot to turn the whole world into a moneygrubbing sweatshop?"

"I'm authorizing the Cetus Project!" said the President.

"When you summarize the matter in those forceful terms, I am compelled to give my approval for the action," said the President, slapping his desk to reinforce the point. One of the drawer-pulls fell off. "I am authorizing Operation Cetacean!"

"Comrade President, I give you my personal assurance that you will not have cause to regret your historic decision," the KGB Chairman declared.

"I recall similar words being spoken when your predecessor proposed that lunatic scheme to fill every square meter of the American Embassy building with 'undetectable' listening devices," the Chief Adviser remarked acidly.

"That was a failure of technology, not of strategy," the KGB Chairman retorted. "How could anyone have possibly foreseen that the circuitry buried throughout the walls would transform the entire building into an enormous radio permanently tuned to a sweet-balalaika music station in Smolensk?"

Woods Hole—May 16

Ishmael went up the stairs to Stacey's condominium two steps at a time, rang the bell, and when she opened the door, he hugged her so eagerly he almost knocked her over in his excitement.

"Dipp just called," he practically shouted. "They've approved the project! They want us to go to the Pacific—both of us! Stace, honey, I understand how you feel about the whales and war and Dipp and all, but you've just got to be there to test the rest of the alphabet the moment we get our hands on it! Please say you'll come along!"

"Yes, yes, of course I'll go," said Stacey, surprising Ishmael with the alacrity of her decision. "I can't refuse a direct order."

"Well, it's really more of a request," said Ishmael, "but I knew you'd say yes! Oh, I'm sure we're going to find those missing pieces! You know, Stacey, in a way the whales brought us together, and it would be nice someday to be able to say to them, in their own language, 'Thanks, big guys!' "

They made passionate love on the thick shag carpet in Stacey's living room . . .

Stacey smiled and kissed him, and in a minute they were making passionate love on the thick shag carpet in her living room. Afterward, as she began packing, Stacey wondered whether, if it ever became necessary, she could ask a whale to kill someone.

Petropavlovsk, U.S.S.R.—May 17

Tanya Melanyin was overcome with pleasure and astonishment. This amazing man was demanding her body for the fourth time in a single night, his powerful hands exploring her curves and hollows with as much thoroughness as they had over two hours earlier, when he had first taken her with an intensity and a passion that told her at once that she would never experience his equal.

The telephone on the night table gave an electronic burp. Colonel Viktor Tiktov picked up the handset, listened for a few moments, then spoke, and although he did not cease his insistent motions with Tanya, nothing in his cold voice betrayed his sexual arousal.

"I will be there in one hour. See that all is in readiness." He hung up the instrument and brought his movements to a crescendo. As he approached his climax, he said something Tanya did not understand since it was in perfect English. She assumed it was some cry of passion, and in a way it was: "So, Dipp Schmidt—we meet again!"

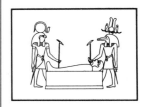

U.S.S. Clive Cussler, *Pearl Harbor—May 17*

Captain Frank Starbuck cursed as he read the orders that had been delivered to the ship moments earlier by a messenger from Fleet Headquarters. His Executive Officer, Lt. Commander Pete Stubb, strolled across the bridge of the Clancy-class frigate.

"Bad news, Skipper?" he asked in the flat accent of his native New Bedford.

"Read it and weep," said Starbuck, handing over the folded sheet of paper. "We're ordered to sail at once for some hunk of gull doo on the Equator called Palmyra Island." In the Captain's Nantucket twang, it came out "Palemirror."

"Why don't they send the *Ludlum* or the *Coonts*?" said Stubb angrily. "We're due a week of shore leave."

"Ours not to reason why, Pete," said Starbuck, "though the little bird that just took a great big dump on our heads tells me that it has something to do with the fact that we're the only friggin' frigate in the Navy equipped with seagoing salvage gear and manned with a full complement of trained scuba divers."

"What's this about making rendezvous with the *Truro*?" asked Stubb, brandishing the movement orders. "That's an Oceanographic Institute research ship I used to see over to Woods Hole. It's got a wooden hull so it can get clear magnetic readings from the sea floor."

"Yeah, well, the way I see it, that's the beauty part," Starbuck groused. "I figure if we're real lucky, we'll get to attend some lectures from a bunch of seal-squeezers and porpoise-patters who want to tell us what bad boys we are for having those nasty old nuclear weapons on board that for the last 40-odd years have protected their inalienable right to call us scumbags."

"Hot diggety," said Stubb. "And to think, we almost got stuck having to spend seven days slopping down mai-tais and checking out the swimsuits on Waikiki."

S.S. Truro, *Palmyra Island—May 18*

Captain John Gardiner sat in his cabin sipping a cup of coffee. It was his fifth of the day and, at least in terms of daylight, the day was only one hour old.

For the umpteenth time, Gardiner reread the telex from the Director of the Institute: "Suspend research on long-term aftereffects of nuclear testing at Johnston Island. Proceed to Palmyra Island to await important visitors. P.S. Frisky had six puppies."

At first glance, the message seemed all too clear. Some political heat had come down on the Institute over the *Truro*'s current voyage to document the severe ecological damage that still remained evident nearly 30 years after a series of atmospheric nuclear weapons tests in the Pacific, and the Director had been pressured to end the project. But the final phrase was part of a simple private code he and the Director had come up with years ago. If something was very urgent, Frisky, an imaginary dog, would have a puppy. When the Air Force lost an H-bomb in deep water off Spain in 1966, the message sending Gardiner to look for it announced the birth of four puppies. Six was by far the largest litter ever produced by the ill-omened pooch.

"Me still no sabee why we come this plenty stinky place," said a voice right next to Gardiner's ear.

The startled captain turned around to see the half-naked Polynesian native whose gift for soundless movement was only surpassed by his extraordinary skills as a navigator, his genuine gifts as a culinary artist, and his uncanny powers of premonition.

"Read it and weep," said Starbuck, handing over the sheet of paper.

"Goddamn it, Queequeg, you're going to give me a heart attack one of these days," Gardiner growled good-naturedly.

"Me no sleepee for shitee," said Queequeg. "Me feel much fella trouble him flyee here now lickety-splittee in big metal birdee."

The *Truro*'s radar operator stuck his head in the door. "Cap'n, I've just picked up the biggest goddamn radar blip I've ever seen, and it's heading our way at Mach 2.5!"

At that moment, a pair of thunderous sonic booms rocked the *Truro*'s sturdy cedar hull, followed by another, even louder pair reflected off the surface of the sea. The three men went out on deck in time to see a huge, but oddly graceful plane pass overhead at 1,000 feet, its movable wings slowly sweeping forward into landing position as it banked to approach the airstrip on the deserted island from the Northeast.

"Is that what I think it is?" asked the radarman.

"Yeah, it's a B-1 bomber," Gardiner replied. He had a feeling Frisky was going to end up providing him with enough puppies to fill a whole kennel.

2

Lt. Colonel Hack Flemington braked the giant plane to a stop 100 feet short of the end of the cracked concrete runway and turned to the three passengers jammed into the seats normally occupied by the ECM officer, the Terminal Target Guidance Specialist, and the Bombardier. He felt it was appropriate that the Bombardier's chair had been used by the gorgeous brunette—after all, she was one bombshell. She had turned a bit green, and the sandy-haired kid looked a little sick, too, but Dipp Schmidt was busily doing calculations on a pad strapped to the leg of his G-suit.

"Well, Hack old boy," said Dipp cheerfully, "you can chalk up another world record: from Andrews to here in 4 hours, 51 minutes, 11 seconds, including two midair refuelings. Too bad we can't send it in to *The Guinness Book of Records.*"

"Yep," said Flemington. "It would have looked real nice next to another missing entry—your record for the fastest flight from Omsk to Oslo in a stolen MiG-29."

Dipp flipped the grizzled Air Force officer a salute and went down the steep ladder that unfolded from the plane's belly hatch, then helped Ishmael and Stacey as they followed him unsteadily on the narrow titanium stairway. As soon as they reached the ground, Dipp hurried them off the runway and flashed a thumbs-up sign toward the cockpit. The bomber, its engines still idling, immediately began rolling into position for takeoff, and 45 seconds later, it shot into the already hot tropical morning air with a deafening roar, heading northwest toward Guam, the only stop that would ever appear on its official flight plan.

As the plane rapidly diminished in size, one of the *Truro*'s inflatable Zodiac boats scraped to a stop on the beach that ran along the very edge of the World War II airstrip, and Dipp, Stacey, and Ishmael, blinking in the dazzling Pacific sunlight, headed for the rubber craft.

The entire procedure had taken only seven minutes, but that was enough time for a Soviet nuclear-powered *Yenta* Naval Intelligence Satellite in stationary orbit 540 kilometers over Hawaii to take five pictures, of which two were of outstanding clarity.

Gardiner's expression was one of mingled astonishment and relief when he saw who his "important visitors" were.

"Ishmael! Stacey Romano! What in hell is going on? And Jesus Christ, Dipp Schmidt! Welcome aboard!"

"Me feel much fella trouble him flyee here now in big metal birdee," said Queequeg.

"Hello, Johnny-boy," said Dipp, shaking Gardiner's hand warmly. "Seen any mermaids lately?"

"You two know each other!" Ishmael blurted in surprise as the boat pulled away from the beach.

"Yeah, we did a little salvage job together a few years back," said Gardiner, as he opened up the throttles on the Zodiac's twin 50 hp outboard motors. "A Nazi submarine sank off Buenos Aires in June of 1945, and we wanted to find out whether it went down before or after a very special passenger had a chance to get off."

"Oh my God," said Stacey, "Hitler! Did he escape?"

"Well, let's just say you don't need to start taking German lessons," said Dipp lightly. He looked across the tranquil waters of the lagoon, where the *Truro* was anchored. A good-looking female crew member windsurfed into view from behind the boxy shape of the 120-foot research ship and tacked gracefully back and forth, then disappeared again around the vessel's blunt bow. "But if we fail in our present endeavors," he added in a more serious tone, "we're all going to have to start taking Russian lessons."

Stacey made a choking sound, then leaned over the edge of the boat and was sick.

"She hates to fly," said Ishmael, putting a comforting arm around her shoulders.

Dames, thought Dipp. He wished he could violate security to tell her that Hitler's sub had sunk because of a short circuit in its batteries caused by Eva Braun's hair dryer.

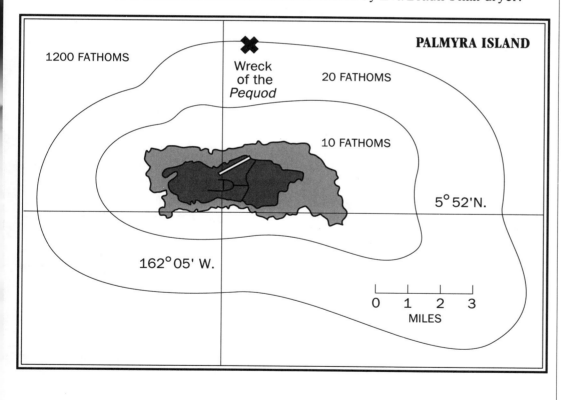

"If we fail," said Dipp, "we're all going to have to start taking Russian lessons."

3

"Raise the *Pequod*?" Captain Gardiner exclaimed in amazement when Dipp finished outlining the Cetus Project to the *Truro*'s small crew in the ship's wardroom. "Finding that old hunk of history has been a dream of mine since boyhood! You see, my great-great-great-grandfather was captain of the *Rachel*!"

"Of course, *Captain Gardiner*!" said Ishmael. "I never put two and two together!"

"It gets better," said Gardiner, walking over to a chart table and unrolling a map of the Pacific on which the last part of the *Pequod*'s voyage had been plotted. "As a hobby, I've played around with every scrap of evidence I could find about the *Pequod*'s course, and I think I can narrow the search area down even further than you have." Gardiner smiled conspiratorially. "To tell you the truth, I planned to make a little detour down here when we finished up at Johnston Island, so I looked up a native islander who knows these waters inside out. I'll ask him to join us."

"You callee for mee?" said Queequeg, who, with his eerie precognition, had anticipated the summons. "Hello, my name Queequeg. What yours?"

"My God, you must be his descendant!" cried Ishmael, his voice cracking with emotion. "Queequeg, I'm Ishmael, great-great-great-grandson of your great-great-great-grandfather's friend on the *Pequod*!"

"Holee Molee!" shouted the 250-pound Polynesian, almost smothering Ishmael in a bone-crushing bear hug.

"Queequeg," said Ishmael when he could breathe again, "we're going to raise the *Pequod*. Can you help us find the wreck?"

The portly native of the South Pacific began to back away towards the door, his bronze face visibly whitening. "N-O-E-E spells Noee!" he shouted. "That wreckee have badee curse—very big fella monster he be there. No go nearee!"

"That's superstitious nonsense," said Dipp. "This is the twentieth century."

"Biggee fuckee deal," said Queequeg. "In nineteenth century, everybody him makee laughee at curse on Ahab, but him still kickee bucket for very damn sure!"

"You've read *Moby-Dick,* Queequeg?" asked Stacey.

"No, but I see movie. Me thinkee Gregory Peck be dopey choice to playee Ahab—Brando be muchee-muchee better."

"Queequeg, help us for the sake of our ancestors' friendship," Ishmael pleaded.

"For they sake, me *no* help you. Me no let monster Pehee-nuee-nuee eat you up."

"I'll help you," said a husky female voice from the wardroom doorway. "I've seen that wreck—I know where it is."

Her trim, brown-skinned body was bare save for a wet bikini.

A stunning young Polynesian girl walked into the room, toweling her auburn hair. Her trim, brown-skinned body was bare save for a wet bikini whose skimpy top barely restrained her firm, full breasts. "Hi, I'm Sheequeg."

Queequeg uttered a few angry phrases in his native tongue. "No, father," said Sheequeg defiantly when he had finished speaking. "I will show them the place, monster or no monster."

Stacey bristled. "The only monster on the sea is man," she declared. "Sheequeg, you don't believe in sea monsters, do you?"

"Yes, I *do* believe in sea monsters," Sheequeg said earnestly, "and I'd give anything for a chance to study one. You see, I have a degree in abnormal marine psychology from the University of Hawaii. I did my thesis on serial killer whales."

"How far is the wreck from here?" Dipp asked.

"About ten miles, near a coral ridge called Devil's Deadman's Haunted Hell Reef."

"You no have to be rocket scientist fella to guessee why it havee namee likee that," said Queequeg ominously.

"How about it, John?" Dipp said to the *Truro*'s captain.

"Be there around lunchtime," the captain replied, and he headed for the bridge.

"Was that you windsurfing?" Dipp said to Sheequeg, giving her the "Brows Raise Like Morning Fog" glance from the Chinese *Eye Ching,* the Book of Meaningful Looks.

"Yes," she answered, her soft brown eyes meeting his.

"Will you teach me some time?"

"Of course. It's very easy. It's all in the hips."

Dipp slowly moved his gaze from her shapely loins and taut belly to her chest, where the outline of her hard nipples pressed against the thin bathing-suit material. *Well, there's a lot of it in the hips,* Dipp thought, *but there's some of it in a few other places, too.*

International Date Line—May 19

"We're about to cross the Date Line, Colonel," said Captain Konakovsky with ill-disguised relief. "We'll pick up a whole day!" Thank God they were heading east! Without the artificial time gain, they never could have met the punishing schedule set by the notoriously short-tempered and influential KGB colonel, and Konakovsky did not relish the prospect of spending the rest of his career on an icebreaker in the Arctic.

International Date Line—May 18

"Good work, Captain," replied Tiktov. "We should arrive in plenty of time to give the Americans a *whale* of a surprise."

Devil's Deadman's Haunted Hell Reef—May 18

"Yow!" yelped the crewman operating the *Truro*'s undersea metal-detection array. He took off his headset, massaged his ears, and adjusted the sensitivity knob. "Captain," he called out, "either some clown just tied an anvil to my fucking Ferrous Substance Sensor Probe or there's about a ton of cast iron less than 60 feet below us!"

"Sir, I'm getting a seesaw reading between ten fathoms and 1,200 fathoms," the sonar operator reported.

"We're over the edge of the underwater reef," said Gardiner. "We'll take her 500 yards into the shallow basin area and drop anchor."

"Aye-aye," the helmsman confirmed.

Dipp came onto the bridge at a trot. "Paydirt?" he asked.

"Bingo," said Gardiner. "Sheequeg was just about right on the money. We'd have found it a couple of hours ago, but it looks like some sort of tidal action has eaten away at the abyssal wall since she first saw the wreck when she was diving out here last year, and now it's much closer to the edge."

"We've got another few hours of daylight," said Dipp. "I'm going down for a look."

2

Even in the diminished illumination provided by the oblique rays of the afternoon sun, the outline of the 100-foot long wooden sailing ship sitting nearly upright in the white bottom sand no more than 50 yards from the black depths of the abyss was clearly visible almost from the moment Dipp and two of the *Truro*'s divers slipped below the surface of the warm tropical water.

Dipp slowly moved his gaze from her shapely loins and taut belly to her chest . . .

The skeleton of a man was hanging out of one of the giant iron trypots . . .

A few minutes of slow, steady swimming brought them parallel to the sunken vessel's upper deck, and they began a clockwise reconnaissance of the wreck. As they swam, they could feel the powerful current tugging them toward the sharp drop-off at the edge of the coral reef.

Except for a large hole in the starboard bow, the ship was surprisingly intact. All three of the masts were broken off not far above the deck, and spars and masses of debris clogged its upper surfaces, but the hull was remarkably clean and free of marine growth.

The three divers paused at the stern. Four of the six elaborately carved letters that had once adorned it were still there: P QUO . Chiseled into a plank just below them was the still legible word: NANTUCKET.

One of the *Truro*'s divers tapped Dipp on the shoulder, then tapped his watch and pointed upward. Dipp nodded. The air in their tanks was being rapidly depleted under the pressure of the deep water, and they would need time to decompress during the ascent. As they began their slow, careful return to the surface, Dipp paused for a moment at the ship's stern rail and worked loose a piece of wood. As he did so, he saw in the deepening gloom the outline of one of the giant iron trypots that had triggered the *Truro*'s metal detector. The skeleton of a man was hanging out of it.

3

"That was delicious, Queequeg," said Captain Gardiner as he surveyed the clean plates on the galley's dinner table. "You really outdid yourself." There were enthusiastic murmurs of agreement from Dipp, Ishmael, Stacey, and the *Truro*'s crew.

"Me happy you likee," said Queequeg sourly. "Me thinkee it our last mealee, so me makee special dishee." He got up and left, whistling some weird, tuneless dirge. Sheequeg made an apologetic gesture and followed him.

"Well, here's where we stand," said Gardiner. "I did some calculations, and the way that current is shifting and undermining the sands, the wreck will fall off the edge of the reef and into the abyss within two days at the most. What it comes down to is that we have no choice—either we raise the *Pequod* immediately, or we lose it forever."

"It's a damn good thing we didn't waste any time filing an Environmental Impact Statement," said Dipp sarcastically. "By the time we'd found out that we weren't about to disturb the only known habitat of a colony of Asymmetrically Serrated Slimeballs, the *Pequod* would have been at the bottom of a mile of seawater and about as salvageable as a Popsicle from a pitbull's mouth."

The *Truro*'s marine archaeologist held up the piece of the *Pequod*'s rail that Dipp had taken from the wreck. "We've got a real problem here," he said. "The reason why the hull has very little rot or major visible decay and none of the usual infestations of destructive organisms is that there's probably a rift vent at the bottom of the abyss that's leaking out a huge volume of dissolved minerals from a crustal fracture point. It's basically an undersea volcano. Now, at great depths, it supports some bizarre life forms, like tube worms, but up here in the shallow water, it inhibits the growth of flora and fauna."

"That all sounds like good news to me," said Dipp. "If it hadn't been for that mineral effect, the wreck would be a heap of slime-encrusted mush."

"Agreed," said the scientist, "but over the years, the *Pequod*'s wood has become thoroughly mineralized. It's basically rock at this point—it's heavy, and it's brittle." He dropped the piece of the *Pequod* on the table. It landed with a thud that rattled the dishes.

"In other words," said Gardiner, "she can't be raised with cables and conventional

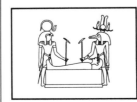

lifting gear. She'll have to be floated.''

''You can forget about pumping her full of air,'' said one of the crew members who had been on the drive with Dipp. ''Even if we cover the hatches and patch the hole in the hull, the planks have shrunk so much there are half-inch gaps everywhere.''

''We can't just sit here and watch her be swept into the depths!'' Ishmael cried. ''We've got to save the *Pequod*!''

''Maybe—maybe it's for the best if the *Pequod* sinks beyond our reach,'' said Stacey somberly. ''After all, that ship brought nothing but death to whales and her crew.''

''Oh, Stacey, you can't mean that,'' Ishmael protested. ''Think of the potential benefit to mankind and, um, whalekind if we find what we're looking for! Oh, there must be some way to raise the *Pequod*!''

''Well, I can't help you—I'm just a humble diesel mechanic,'' said one of the crew members. ''Anyone for Ping-Pong?''

''You're on,'' said the sonar operator, and the two men headed for the *Truro*'s recreation room.

''My God, that's it!'' Dipp shouted. ''We may be up shit's creek, but we *do* have a paddle,'' he added cryptically as he made his way toward the ship's radio room.

U.S.S. Clive Cussler—*May 18*

Captain Starbuck delicately passed the black silk thread into the miniature block and tackle on the mizzen boom of the model of an 1840-era whaling ship. Years earlier, he had discovered that constructing painstaking replicas of historic sailing vessels was the best way to take his mind off the burdens of command. As invariably happened whenever he began any really delicate work, there was a knock on his stateroom door.

''Come in,'' he said crossly.

Lt. Commander Stubb stepped in, a big smile on his face. ''I hate to disturb you, Skipper, but this news is too good to wait.'' He handed Starbuck a radio message.

Soon a grin passed over the Captain's leathery features as well. ''So, Dipp Schmidt is on the *Truro*! Well, this could turn out to be not so bad after all.''

''Yeah, and I know her skipper, John Gardiner. He's another Nantucket man—and a top-notch sea captain.''

''What's this Naval Supply System Item Number refer to?'' Starbuck wondered.

''Beats me, Captain. But whatever it is, Dipp wants a hell of a lot of them fast, and he has an 'Ultra' priority.''

''O.K., Pete, contact Pearl. Get those procurement bozos out of bed and order them to fill this requisition ASAP. Have the chopper jockeys line up a Sea Stallion to ferry the stuff out here and inform them that we'll be ready to take delivery on our fantail helicopter pad at first light. And tell Dipp we'll have his goodies with us when we rendezvous with the *Truro* at 1100 hours tomorrow.''

When Stubb had left to wreak some havoc in the Fleet Supply Center at Pearl Harbor, Starbuck put down his miniature rigging tools and sat back in his chair. *Dipp Schmidt, you old pirate,* he thought, *what are you up to now?* He smiled as he remembered the look on the North Korean boarding party commander's face when Schmidt had kicked him in the nuts at the exact moment the false bulkheads of the decoy spy ship *Alamo* had dropped and a barrage of six-inch shells and antiship rockets had torn four commie patrol boats and a destroyer into scrap metal in two minutes flat.

That was the nice thing about Dipp. He didn't play by the rules.

"My God, that's it!" Dipp shouted. "We may be up shit's creek, but we do have a paddle!"

Devil's Deadman's Haunted Hell Reef—May 19

The *Truro* was a well-run ship, but she was not a naval vessel. The crew stood watches, but the radio room was not manned 24 hours a day. The person who slipped in at 3:15 A.M. found it empty and unguarded. The message took less than a minute to send. It consisted of four number groups: 9-12-173-28. By themselves, they were meaningless. But if from each number group another number was subtracted based on the place in the alphabet of the first four letters of the first word of a certain novel, the numbers gave the exact latitude and longitude of the *Truro*'s position: 6°11′ N., 162°17′ W.

2

Captain Gardiner stood on the bridge and watched the last few hundred yards of the one-inch sampling nets disappear over the side. The *Truro* carried nearly a mile of the intricately woven dacron polyfilament mesh which it used to capture fish for research purposes. Since dawn, $900,000 worth of the nets had been wrapped around the hulk of the *Pequod* by relay teams of divers, and he still didn't have the slightest idea what Dipp was up to. Worse still, at the rate the currents were eroding the edge of Devil's Deadman's Haunted Hell Reef, the *Pequod,* cocooned in his precious nets, would be lost forever before nightfall.

"Captain, I have a contact bearing 012°, seven miles out," said the radar operator.

"That must be the *Cussler,*" said Gardiner.

"I have a contact, too," said the sonar man, "but it's not propeller noise. It's a low rumbling sound, sort of like a subterranean hum."

"Where's it coming from?"

"From somewhere below the reef wall, Skipper—down at the bottom of the abyss."

Dipp ran his hand along Sheequeg's back to the string that fastened her bikini top . . .

"Contact the *Nauset.* Tell Dipp the *Cussler*'s here and that our sonar has picked something up—they may have company down there," Gardiner said to the radioman.

He hadn't been crazy about letting Dipp and Sheequeg take the *Truro*'s minisub to explore the reef wall to see if there was any chance that the wreck of the *Pequod* might land safely on a lower shelf if it went over the edge, but he hadn't had any choice. The sub only carried two, Dipp knew how to drive it, and Sheequeg knew the waters like the back of her hand.

3

It was surprisingly warm and humid in the cramped cockpit of the *Nauset,* and even though Dipp and Sheequeg wore only their bathing suits, they were both perspiring freely. Through the thick viewport, the sheer rocky walls of the edge of Devil's Deadman's Haunted Hell Reef dropped off sharply into an inky blackness that even the minisub's powerful halogen searchlight couldn't penetrate.

"Roger," said Dipp when the call came in from the *Truro*. "We're heading up now. And tell Gardiner it's no dice—if the *Pequod* goes over, she's lost for good. Out." Dipp switched off the radio.

Sheequeg tensed. "That hum the sonar man picked up—I think I can hear it."

Dipp listened. Over the smooth whine of the minisub's electric motor, there was a barely discernible hum of varying pitch, sometimes very low, sometimes well above

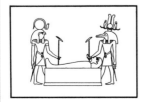

human hearing. "That doesn't sound like any submarine I've ever heard," he said. "I wonder what the hell it is?"

"I think it may be the monster," said Sheequeg quietly.

"Sheequeg, do you really believe that claptrap?"

"Dipp, have you ever met a man who was totally evil—a psychopathic killer?"

Dipp thought immediately of Viktor Tiktov. "Yeah, I think I know the type."

"Well, there's no difference between aquatic animals and humans. Some of them become consumed by pathological hatred and turn into killing machines. In marine psychology we call them 'seacopaths'—superstitious people like my father call them 'sea monsters.' It adds up to the same thing."

Dipp set the minisub's controls for an automatic ascent to the surface.

"I beg to differ," said Dipp, running his hand along Sheequeg's moist back to the string that fastened her bikini top. "I think there are some differences between aquatic animals and humans, and *vive la différence.*" He pulled on the ties and slipped the little piece of cloth off her firm, swelling breasts revealing her large, erect nipples.

"Oh, Dipp, I want you," Sheequeg moaned, and as the minisub slowly rose, it was rocked back and forth by the strong currents that flowed outside its aluminum hull and the equally powerful surging motions that shook it from within.

4

"Ping-Pong balls!" Captain Starbuck shouted into the radio as he looked aft from the bridge of the *Cussler* to the frigate's fantail, where crew members were starting to unload the large metal container the Navy helicopter had gingerly deposited on the ship's deck just after dawn. Lt. Commander Stubb held in his hand one of the light, hollow, white plastic spheres that filled the huge steel box. "Dipp, what the heck is going on?"

"Easy, Frank," came Dipp's reply from the *Truro*. "They may *look* like Ping-Pong balls, but they're actually Individual Spherical Flotation Units. The Navy paid $43.22 apiece for them. I want your divers to run hoses from your compressors down to the *Pequod* and pump her full of those ISFUs. They'll give that wreck the buoyancy it needs to rise up off the bottom, and they can't slip out of the cracks between her sprung planks or through the one-inch mesh of the netting that's covering every opening in her hull."

Starbuck rolled his eyes. "Dipp, if you ever tell anyone I had anything to do with this loony scheme, I'll boil you in oil!"

"Frank, trust me," Dipp's voice crackled from the radio. "After all, did I ever tell a soul about that plan to put a bomb in the toy sub in Qaddafi's Jacuzzi?"

Pete Stubb gave his commanding officer a quizzical look.

"You heard the man," Starbuck snapped. "Let's rig those hoses."

5

The television monitor on the *Truro*'s bridge showed a clear black and white picture of the feverish activity on the sea floor below taken from the nose camera of the *Nauset,* from which Captain Gardiner was supervising the injection of the Ping-Pong balls into the *Pequod.* As Dipp watched, a large section of the sandy bottom on which the old wreck rested slid soundlessly into the abyss, leaving the still immobile hulk less than ten yards from the edge of the undersea chasm.

He pulled on the ties and slipped the piece of cloth off her firm, swelling breasts . . .

"Oh, Dipp, I want you," Sheequeg moaned.

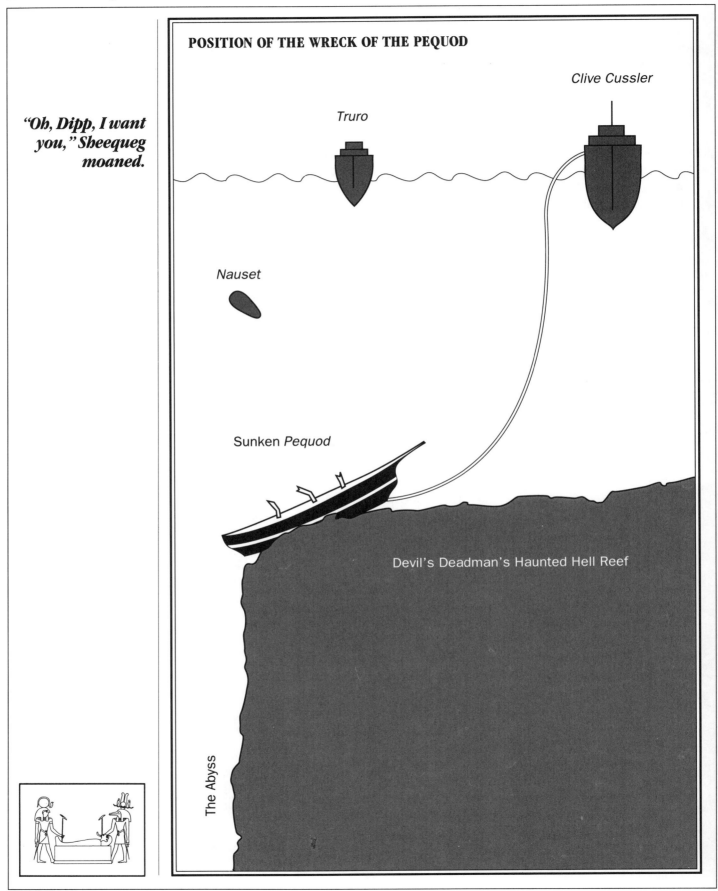

POSITION OF THE WRECK OF THE PEQUOD

Clive Cussler

Truro

Nauset

Sunken *Pequod*

Devil's Deadman's Haunted Hell Reef

The Abyss

Dipp punched the transmit button on the radio. "Frank, the moment the *Pequod* breaks the surface, I'm going aboard her. I don't know how long she'll stay afloat."

"If she comes up at all," said Starbuck. "The last Ping-Pong—I mean ISFUs—are being pumped in right now and she hasn't budged an inch."

"She'll come up," said Dipp firmly. "Have a team ready to secure her with cables. I want you to tow her into shallower waters just as fast as you can so that if she sinks again, we'll get another chance to raise her."

"O.K., Dipp—will do. By the way, our sonar is picking up some strange sounds from the deep zone."

"Yeah, we heard those, too. Some folks over here think it's a sea monster, but I figure it's just some volcanic activity."

"The only monster around here is the humongous bill the Navy is going to have to pay for this little escapade," said Starbuck.

Dipp smiled. He had signed Admiral Chairweather's name to the $43,220,000 requisition order.

The strip of reef the **Pequod** *had rested on dropped away, revealing the sensuous curve of her keel . . .*

6

"But that's fantastic," said Sheequeg after Stacey and Ishmael had explained the basics of whale communication. "Your discovery means that we can explore the minds of creatures who face an entirely different array of emotional challenges."

"Like being netted, hooked, and harpooned," said Stacey sadly. "I think they'd have every right to hate us."

Dipp leaned in the wardroom doorway. "Sorry to interrupt the interspecies consciousness-raising session, but our *Pequod*-raising session is about to get started. Ishmael, get the Zodiac boat ready. If the strain of being yanked off the bottom is too much for her proud but superannuated planks, the *Pequod* may begin to break up as soon as she hits the surface. We might only have a few minutes to find what we're searching for."

"Ishmael, I'm coming with you," said Stacey determinedly. "I want to be a part of Operation Cetacean, from start to finish."

Dipp gave Stacey a quizzical glance. "O.K. by me," he said. "Sheequeg?"

Queequeg slipped silently into the wardroom, his face ashen. "You wakee Peheenuee-nuee," he said in a hoarse whisper. "Pehee-nuee-nuee, him come now. Him come now and him killee allee people."

"I better stay with him," said Sheequeg.

7

On the TV monitor on the *Truro*'s bridge, the wreck of the *Pequod* sat motionless in the sand. The thick rubber hoses that had fed the Ping-Pong balls into her holds had been removed, and the last divers were slowly ascending. Suddenly, the entire strip of reef on which the hull had rested for 150 years dropped away into the abyss, revealing for the first time in a century and a half the full, almost sensuous curve of her long-buried, copper-sheathed keel.

Dipp held his breath as the hulk of the old whaling ship remained suspended in midwater, like a cartoon character who has run off the edge of a cliff and not yet looked down. But unlike that cartoon character, it did not fall. Slowly, almost imperceptibly,

"That's no whale," Dipp snarled. "That's a Soviet nuclear submarine!"

the *Pequod* began to rise.

"Come on, you gorgeous old tub of timbers!" Dipp shouted. "You can do it, baby!"

"She's coming up, Dipp!" Captain Starbuck's voice boomed from the radio. "That beautiful hunk of crud is going to be topside, off your starboard bow, in about a minute!"

Dipp grabbed a walkie-talkie and headed for the *Truro*'s landing stair, where Ishmael and Stacey sat in the Zodiac, its powerful outboards idling throatily. Dipp jumped in, took the helm, and headed the rubber boat toward a spot halfway between the *Truro* and the *Cussler*.

At that moment, two things happened simultaneously. The dark, salt-streaked hull of the *Pequod* burst into sight, and at the same instant, a huge black shape surfaced from the deep waters and began heading toward the point where the wreck was floating, upright and nearly level, its three mast stumps pointing into the air.

"My God, that's the biggest whale I've ever seen!" Ishmael gasped.

"It's Queequeg's monster!" Stacey cried.

Dipp whipped out a pair of binoculars and read the Cyrillic lettering on the bulbous nose of the ominous leviathan. "That's no whale, and it's no sea monster, either," he snarled. "That's a Soviet Bravo-class nuclear submarine!"

Dipp pointed the Zodiac boat at the *Pequod* and opened the throttle all the way. "Starbuck, we've got company!" he shouted into the walkie-talkie. "Those devious commie bastards! That's why we couldn't track that sub! They've developed a silent hydraulic propulsion system based on the up-and-down tail motions of the whales, and they designed the hulls of their boats to resemble the hump-shaped body of a sperm whale so if the Navy ever spots one on the surface, it's logged in as a whale sighting! Hell, they probably even cruise with schools of the giant marine mammals so our sonars lose them in the background noises whales make! Now we know what those weird sounds were we've been picking up on our sonars all day," he added bitterly.

"Negative, we're still picking those up," came Starbuck's reply over the portable radio. "There may be another of those subs hanging around here. We also just got a radio transmission from this one. They identified themselves as the *Prolonged Stormy Applause* on a scientific expedition called 'Operation Cetacean' and warned us away from the *Pequod*—they're claiming they found her first. By the way, how the fuck *did* they find us, Dipp?"

Dipp's face was transformed into an icy mask of hate. "Tell your boarding party to get a move on, Starbuck," he growled into the radio. "We're not giving the *Pequod* up without a fight."

As he spoke, Dipp saw a hatch open in the upper surface of the Soviet submarine, and several of its crewmen jumped out and began inflating a large rubber raft. At the same time, one of the *Cussler*'s boats pulled away from the frigate's stern and headed for the *Pequod* at top speed, paying out towing cable as it went.

Dipp maneuvered the Zodiac alongside the hull of the *Pequod,* and Ishmael, with a practiced skill that came from years of living in a seaport, leapt nimbly on board and tied the craft securely to a remaining piece of the wreck's siderail.

Dipp and Stacey followed Ishmael onto the slimy, net-wrapped deck. "Ishmael, you know the layout of the *Pequod* and you know what we're looking for," Dipp rasped. "Start searching, and I'll try to hold off our Russian friends."

Ishmael took out a pocketknife and began cutting his way through the mesh of the netting to the hatch that led to the captain's cabin. In a moment, he had disappeared through the narrow passageway. Stacey started to follow him, but Dipp grabbed her arm.

"Not so fast, Stacey," Dipp spat. "I want to keep an eye on you—something I should

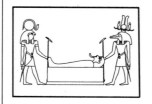

have been doing all along.''

"What—what do you mean, Dipp?'' she stammered.

"You're a KGB agent, aren't you?'' Dipp demanded harshly.

Stacey looked as though she had been slapped, then she began to cry. "Yes, yes I am,'' she sobbed. "How did you find out?''

"You referred to our efforts to raise the *Pequod* as 'Operation Cetacean.' That's the commie name for the identical plan they put together with your help. *We* call it the 'Cetus Project.' Remember?''

"Oh, Dipp, I didn't want to help them. You've got to believe me,'' Stacey begged. "They made me do it. You see, even though I was raised in America, I am Russian. My mother defected when I was a baby and took me with her, but my father could not escape. They will kill him if I do not do as they say.''

"So your name isn't Stacey Romano,'' Dipp said coldly.

"No. It is Anastasia Romanov,'' said Stacey.

"Then you're the daughter of Grand Duke Nicholas! You're the missing Czarina!''

Stacey's mouth dropped open in astonishment. "You have met my father?''

"A tall, thin man, with a sharp chin, a birthmark on the back of his left hand, and a limp in his right leg from three toes he lost to frostbite during the seige of Leningrad?''

"It is him! Where is he? Is he alive? You must tell me!'' Stacey cried. Dipp began to answer, but just then, within seconds of each other, the American and Russian boarding parties scrambled onto the *Pequod,* the Americans from the ship's stern, the Russians from the bow. Several of the sailors in each group were armed with automatic weapons, and both parties immediately began attaching towing cables to their respective parts of the wreck.

At the head of the group of Russians a slender, cruel-faced figure with fiery eyes stepped forward. "Greetings, Commander Schmidt,'' said Colonel Viktor Tiktov.

Dipp looked at his old adversary with loathing. "Hello, Viktor,'' he said evenly. He turned to Stacey. "Your father died in my arms in Gorky Park in Moscow on September 17, 1984,'' he said quietly. He gave a barely perceptible nod of his head toward Tiktov. "That is the man who shot him.''

A murderous look passed over Stacey's face. "Promise me he will die,'' she hissed.

"That's an easier pledge to make than to swear to give up liver and spinach for life,''

"Promise me he will die," Stacey hissed.

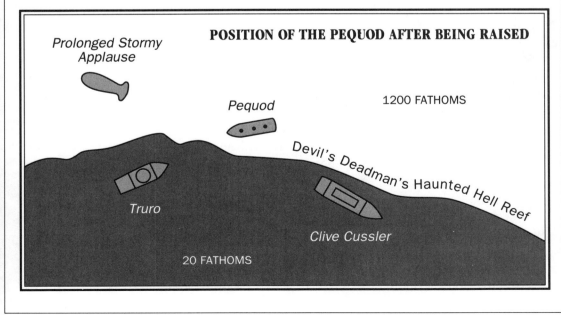

POSITION OF THE PEQUOD AFTER BEING RAISED

Prolonged Stormy Applause

Pequod

1200 FATHOMS

Devil's Deadman's Haunted Hell Reef

Truro

Clive Cussler

20 FATHOMS

said Dipp, squeezing her hand.

Ishmael reappeared at the top of the gangway. "Stacey, I heard everything," he said, his voice full of hurt. "You don't love me—you were just using me."

"No, Ishmael, it isn't true," Stacey protested tearfully.

"O.K. you two, let's save the waterworks for the Geraldo show on 'Men Who Love Spies,'" Dipp ordered. "Any luck, Ishmael?" he inquired under his breath.

Ishmael shook his head. "There wasn't time for a thorough search, but I checked all the likely places—Ahab's cabin, the carpenter's workshop, the galley. No sign of the missing pieces anywhere."

"Good Lord, it's Moby-Dick!" cried Ishmael.

"So, Dipp Schmidt, are you prepared to be reasonable, or are we going to have a tug-of-war that will perhaps lead to World War III?" said Tiktov smoothly, making his way down the *Pequod*'s debris-strewn deck toward Dipp. As he spoke, the tow cables from the *Cussler* and the *Applause* snapped tight and the old hulk began to creak and groan as the frigate's propeller and the submarine's huge, flukelike propulsion planes began pulling relentlessly at the prize.

8

U.S.S. Clive Cussler

"Arm the ASROCs," said Captain Starbuck. "Commence the enabling sequence on both Talon batteries. Disengage missile safety switches."

Prolonged Stormy Applause

"Flood tubes one through four," said Captain Konakovsky. "Open outer doors. Prepare a firing solution for two salvos of two torpedoes each."

9

Tiktov bent down and picked up a harpoon that had been jammed for fifteen decades under a fallen spar. Its point, though rusted, still appeared lethal. Dipp looked intently at the weapon's thick shaft, then whispered to Stacey, "Did you tell the KGB about the piece of Ahab's leg?"

"No, I told them as little as possible, the pigs!"

At that instant, the *Pequod* began to vibrate with an ominous humming noise. Tiktov stopped to listen, and both the American and the Russian sailors exchanged puzzled glances among themselves.

Then, suddenly, with a sound that was part the cold howl of a fierce gale and part the thundering roar of a tidal wave, a gigantic white whale leapt almost entirely clear of the water and landed with a titanic splash less than 200 yards from the *Pequod*.

"Good Lord, it's Moby-Dick!" cried Ishmael. "The speculations of the whalemen in Chapter 41 of Melville's book were correct—he *is* immortal!"

After pausing for a moment as if selecting his prey, the huge albino sperm whale turned

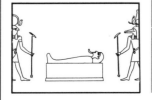

its ponderous head toward the *Truro* and began bearing down on the wooden-hulled oceanographic research ship.

While everyone else on the *Pequod* stood stock-still, virtually paralyzed by the ghastly sight of the terrifying sea creature, Dipp Schmidt sprang into action. "Starbuck," he barked into the walkie-talkie, "get your men off the *Pequod* and back to the *Cussler,* on the double!"

He turned to Stacey and Ishmael. "Get into the Zodiac and go try to talk that hundred-ton honcho into leaving the *Truro* alone! He could crush her like a matchbox!"

"But Dipp, we've only got eight letters of the whale alphabet—how the heck are we going to be able to say anything useful with NOPQRSTU?" Ishmael protested.

"That's *your* problem," Dipp snapped.

"What about you?" said Stacey.

"I've got a little unfinished business to settle here," he said grimly, turning to face Tiktov. "Now move it, you two!"

The *Truro's* rubber boat was tied up on the side of the *Pequod* away from where Moby-Dick had surfaced, and so Stacey and Ishmael had no trouble slipping away while all eyes remained fixed on the immense, milky-hued cetacean.

As Ishmael steered the Zodiac toward the gargantuan alabaster behemoth, his agile mind raced with possible combinations of the pitifully few letters they had to work with, but he was too obsessed with Stacey's treachery to concentrate. "OUT N OUT SNOOP," he said. "NPOSTOR. TURNQUOT."

"No, Ishmael, stop!" Stacey begged. "I didn't mean to hurt you! Please trust me!"

"That's it!" Ishmael shouted. "NO, STOP! TRUST US!"

"TURN!" added Stacey excitedly. "NOT TRURO!"

"SPURN TRURO!" added Ishmael triumphantly.

Hearing the whine of the Zodiac's outboard motors, Moby-Dick altered his course and started approaching the flimsy craft. Stacey immediately began to warble at the colossal lily-white leviathan.

10

With a sharp, supersonic *pop* like a huge bullwhip being cracked, the towline from the *Cussler* snapped and dropped into the water near the stern of the boat that was taking the American crew members back to their ship.

Tiktov smiled. "Well, Dipp, it looks like you lose again," he said in a voice full of malice. He gave a few quick commands in Russian, and the Soviet sailors pointed their guns at Schmidt. "Now, why don't you tell me what we're looking for?" he said menacingly.

Dipp placed his feet firmly on the deck about shoulder width apart, put his thumb against his nose, and began wiggling his fingers in the classic opening posture of Nyah-Nyah, the Gurkah art of getting an opponent's goat by taunting him with carefully chosen traditional Nepalese insults. "Oh you who emerged from the evil-smelling egg of the Owl of Foulness and who are the reincarnation of a thieving, butter-fingered sherpa," Dipp intoned in perfect Russian, "you eat with relish the turds of the mud turtle!"

Tiktov's eyes sparked fire. *Come on, you hot-tempered Ukrainian bastard,* Dipp thought, *throw that harpoon at me!*

"You try my patience, Schmidt," snarled the enraged KGB Colonel.

"You ball of rancid bat dung," Dipp said. "Have you been dipping your syphilitic wick in yaks' assholes again?"

"You try my patience, Schmidt," snarled the enraged KGB colonel.

Tiktov's knuckles tightened around the harpoon handle.

"Instead of the demure sandals that are the appropriate footgear of a woman of high caste," Dipp continued, "your mother is shod in the boots of a common soldier."

Tiktov screamed in fury and, with a powerful overhand throw, sent the harpoon whizzing at Dipp's head. Dipp executed a quick Chinese Food-Boxing maneuver— "The Peking Duck"—and the antique weapon missed him by inches, its rusty point burying itself deep in the dense wood of the jagged base of the *Pequod*'s mizzenmast.

Dipp tugged on the butt of the old whale-spearing tool. The point was jammed fast, but the heavy oak shaft slipped easily out of the corroded metal socket.

"So long, suckers," Dipp cried, and carrying the wooden harpoon handle with him, he jumped over the side of the *Pequod*, propelling himself deep underwater as AK-47 rounds punched into the waves above him.

11

"It's working!" said Ishmael. "He's stopped!"

Moby-Dick sat motionless in the water halfway between the *Truro* and the *Pequod*, a thin veil of mist spouting from the blowhole in his scarred white back.

Stacey looked back toward the *Pequod* just in time to see Dipp go over the side and the Russian sailors begin to fire into the water.

Dipp raised himself out of the water and gave Sheequeg a long, deep kiss.

"The bastards," she hissed between clenched teeth. "They'll pay—for my father and for Dipp." She paused a moment and then started once again to warble.

A look of horror passed over Ishmael's face as he suddenly realized what Stacey was most likely to ask Moby-Dick to do. "No, Stacey, no!" he cried.

Moby-Dick's great eye blinked once, and with a powerful thrust of his gargantuan flukes, he bore down on the *Pequod*. When he hit the side of the old whaling ship, he was traveling at 20 miles an hour and with his 200,000 pounds of mass, the force of the impact was equivalent to a locomotive running broadside into a wooden barn. The *Pequod* exploded into a shower of fragments, and the great shroud of the sea closed over her shattered remains for a second and final time.

12

When Dipp, his lungs bursting from lack of air, finally surfaced, he was amazed to find no trace of the *Pequod*—only a spreading white expanse of Ping-Pong balls through which Sheequeg was adeptly maneuvering her windsurfer.

She swung the sailboard to a perfect stop a yard from Dipp, and he handed her the harpoon handle.

"It looks like I owe your father an apology," said Dipp as he swam alongside. "There really is a monster."

"Pehee-nuee-nuee," said Sheequeg. "It means 'whale' in our language." She frowned. "Unfortunately, it also means 'plenty-plenty-fish,' and, in some contexts, 'Your sofa has exploded.'"

Dipp raised himself out of the water and gave Sheequeg a long, deep kiss. "That means 'thanks for coming to get me' in my language," he said when he reluctantly removed his lips from hers.

Ishmael piloted the Zodiac alongside, and Dipp and Sheequeg got in.

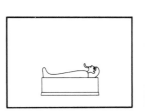

"Dipp, I'm so sorry—I've spoiled everything," said Stacey. "I thought you'd been shot, so I told Moby-Dick to ram the *Pequod* and kill the Russians on deck."

"How did you manage to say that with only those eight letters?" Ishmael marveled.

"PUT SNOUT TO P QUO PRONTO N ROUT RUSS TROOPS ON TOP," Stacey replied. "Fortunately, the 'E' and the 'D' from the *Pequod*'s name were missing from the stern so not having that part of the alphabet wasn't a problem. I guess now NOPQRSTU are the only letters we'll ever have," she added wistfully.

"Read it and don't weep," said Dipp, handing her the harpoon handle. Halfway along its length, it had been mended with a spline of white whalebone in which the letters "A" through "M" were neatly incised, followed by the musical notes representing them in the whale language. "I spotted it as soon as Tiktov picked up the harpoon. It was a billion-to-one shot, like winning the Kentucky Derby with a three-legged horse ridden by a blind, 500-pound jockey seated backward in the saddle, but I decided to go for it!"

"And the other missing letters?" said Ishmael.

"No problem. We have 'U' so we can make a crude double 'U,' for 'V' we can get away with an 'F' sound, 'X' is just 'KS,' for 'Y' we can use 'I,' and 'S' is basically interchangeable with 'Z.' Stacey will have a heavy accent for a while, but the whales will understand her well enough for her to be able to ask them to teach her the missing letters."

"My God, Moby-Dick is going after the Russian submarine!" Sheequeg cried. The huge whale was swimming rapidly toward its mechanical look-alike, which had closed its hatches and was starting to dive.

"Go ahead, you handsome hunk of blubber," Dipp shouted. "Sink that fucker!"

"If my reading of Moby-Dick's psychology is correct, he has something a little different in mind, though it may produce the same result," said Sheequeg.

"What do you mean?"

"Moby-Dick is a sexual psychopath," said Sheequeg. "I think he wants to 'fuck that sinker.'"

13

Eight hundred fathoms and still descending," said the sonar man on the bridge of the *Cussler*. Dipp, Ishmael, Stacey, and Sheequeg stood with Starbuck and Stubb watching the computer-generated display of the edge of Devil's Deadman's Haunted Hell Reef and the abyssal sea floor 22,000 feet below. The joined blips of Moby-Dick and the Russian submarine it was driving into the depths were steadily descending on the screen.

"No missile submarine ever built can withstand that pressure," said Captain Starbuck.

"Implosion," said the sonar man softly, and one of the blips evaporated. The other one circled briefly, then began to rise, shrinking as it did so.

"He's headed away from us at a pretty good clip," said Dipp. "That's the last we'll see of him . . . for *now*."

Stacey turned to Ishmael, leaned over, and whispered something in his ear. He smiled and nodded, and they slipped away, got into the Zodiac, and motored over to a palm-fringed beach on one of the little deserted islands that were dotted here and there along the reef. Ishmael pulled the rubber boat up onto the wave-flattened sand and took Stacey in his arms.

"Say it again, Stacey."

"Ball me, Ishmael."

EPILOGUE

U.S.S. Herman Melville, *North Atlantic—November 5*

The *Hawthorne*-class guided-missile destroyer *Melville* was the first ship in the Navy to be equipped with the computerized ultrasonic broadcast unit, developed by Ishmael, called SCRIMSHAW, the System for Communicating Reliably with Intelligent Mammals of the Sea by High-Frequency Automated Warbler, programmed with the top-secret "Jonah" whale-language tapes prepared by Stacey Romano.

During a routine NATO antisubmarine warfare exercise, the *Melville*, operating with the assistance of the whales code-named "Peter," "Victor," "Dexter," "Daisy," "Daphne," and "Vince," had positively identified and silently tracked 31 Soviet submarines, almost three times the number detected on the sonars of her conventionally equipped escorts, the Royal Navy frigates H.M.S. *Follet* and H.M.S. *Forsyth*.

During the final day of the maneuvers, in waters off the western coast of Ireland designated Control Zone Crystal, the following cetacean transmission was recorded:

PETER: Hey, what the kelp? Where's that old wreck?

VINCE: Beats the ambergris out of me. It's been here for ages.

VICTOR: My cod, look! There's tracks in the muck! Somebody towed that thing away underwater!

DEXTER: What clam-brain would pull a damn-fool stunt like that?

DAISY: Yoo-hoo, *Melville*, are you there?

MELVILLE: We hear you loud and clear.

DAPHNE: What's about 1,000 feet long and weighs as much as Daisy and isn't here anymore?

DAISY: Very funny.

VICTOR: *Melville*, the wreck of the German battleship *Bismarck* is gone—someone has stolen the *Bismarck*!

"What clam-brain would pull a damn-fool stunt like that?" wondered the whale called Dexter.

**Read the exciting sequel to *Moby-Dick II: Raise the Pequod!*
*Moby-Dick III: Resink the Bismarck!***

Raise the Pequod is the first of a projected multivolume collection of fast-paced, edge-of-your-seat sequels to classic but sometimes stuffy works by our nation's greatest writers. This publishing program was recently undertaken by the American Sequel Society in an effort to promote a greater awareness of our literary heritage. The next two titles in the series will be *The Walden Ultimatum*, the riveting story of an attempt by the Chinese to slip a miniature ballistic missile submarine up the Merrimac and Concord rivers and into Thoreau's famous pond, and *The House of the Seven Nuclear Devices*, in which narco-terrorists take over the Salem home of an MIT physicist and hold his family hostage in order to force him to build them a number of deadly atomic bombs.

THE END

The Idiot I: *The Idiot* • The Idiot II: *The Imbecile* • The Idiot III: *The Moron* • The Idiot IV: *The Cretin* • The Idiot V: *The Lamebrain* • The Idiot VI: *The Dimbulb* • The Idiot VII: *The Nitwit* • The Idiot VIII: *The Fathead* • The Idiot IX: *The Numbskull* • The Idiot X: *The Dumb Bunny* • The Idiot XI: *The Yo-Yo* • The Idiot XII: *The Dolt* • The Idiot XIII: *The Clod* • The Idiot XIV: *The Chump* • The Idiot XV: *The Sap* • The Idiot XVI: *The Dunce* • The Idiot XVII: *The Boob* • The Idiot XVIII: *The Dope* • The Idiot XIX: *The Ninny* • The Idiot XX: *The Nincompoop*

"...a...massive...undertaking..."

—*The New York Review of Sequels*

Announcing
THE COMPLETE SET OF SEQUELS TO DOSTOYEVSKY'S *THE IDIOT*

Serious students of Russian literature have long lamented the fact that Fyodor Dostoyevsky's financial difficulties and the demands of his large family denied him the leisure he would have required to write even a single sequel to his favorite work, *The Idiot.* And although the celebrated Russian novelist never did, in fact, have time to continue his magnum opus, there can be no doubt that, given the opportunity, he would have returned to treat at much greater length the moving story of the simpleminded Prince Myshkin.

But would Dostoyevsky have contented himself with simply writing one or two sequels to a book for which he had outlined *eight* complete and separate thematic plans before settling on one to implement in the final version? Or would he have become caught up by the sweep and the grandeur of his original conception and therefore have created a multivolume masterwork as bold, generous, and heroically scaled as Russia herself?

The Most Ambitious Sequel Series of All Time

The answer, we felt, was clear, and clear, too, was our obligation to fill a huge blank space on mankind's bookshelf caused not by a writer's creative failure but by unfortunate circumstances beyond his control. And this same sense of literary duty led directly to our epochal decision to commission *nineteen* complete sequels to *The Idiot,* each one of a quality so high and a style so faithful that Dostoyevsky himself would have been proud to put his name on it.

Take The Fathead *free and* The Imbecile *at our Subscriber's Discount*

Let us send you two volumes from this extraordinary set: *The Imbecile,* the very first sequel to *The Idiot,* and *The Fathead,* one of the later titles in the series that will let you judge the richness and diversity of the collection. And unlike Dostoyevsky, whose compulsive gambling complicated his affairs, you have no risk! You need not buy any future volumes, and you may return *The Imbecile* within 15 days and owe nothing. Mail in the coupon today.

The Idiot I: The Idiot • The Idiot II: The Imbecile • The Idiot III: The Moron • The Idiot IV: The Cretin • The Idiot V: The Lamebrain • The Idiot VI: The Dimbulb • The Idiot VII: The Nitwit • The Idiot VIII: The Fathead • The Idiot IX: The Numbskull • The Idiot X: The Dumb Bunny • The Idiot XI : The Yo-Yo • The Idiot XII: The Dolt • The Idiot XIII: The Clod • The Idiot XIV: The Chump • The Idiot XV: The Sap • The Idiot XVI: The Dunce • The Idiot XVII: The Boob • The Idiot XVIII: The Dope • The Idiot XIX: The Ninny • The Idiot XX: The Nincompoop

---

Ⅱ The American Sequel Society

Yes! Please send me two volumes from this distinguished collection of sequels to *The Idiot—The Fathead* and *The Imbecile.* I may keep *The Fathead* free and pay only for *The Imbecile* at the subscriber's discount price of $5.95. If I decide to subscribe to this important series, I will receive a new volume every month, beginning with *The Moron,* which I will have the option of purchasing for only $24.95. I understand that I may cancel at any time and that if I decide to return *The Imbecile,* I still get to keep *The Fathead* absolutely free!

☐ I am enclosing $5.95
☐ Charge my ☐ Visa ☐ MasterCard

Card No._____ Exp. date_____

Name_____

Address_____

City_____

State_____ Zip_____

TAKE *THE FATHEAD* FREE AND *THE IMBECILE* AT OUR SUBSCRIBER'S DISCOUNT

Culture: The Next Generation

The sequel—as previously noted—is hardly a recent development: its proud tradition dates from the ninth century B.C., when Homer penned *The Odyssey.* The licensing of intellectual property—"liberating" it, in effect, to sire whole new generations of creative products—is, however, a thoroughly modern concept. And as we stand at the gateway to the third millennium, comics, calendars, video games, and theme parks based on preexisting masterpieces are consistently demonstrating a power to inspire and delight rivaling, if not surpassing, that of their progenitors. Indeed, in the very deepest sense, the spin-offs on the following pages represent the embodiment of "Culture: The Next Generation."

**THE STRANGE CASE OF
DR. JEKYLL AND MR. HECKLE**
Sometimes the marriage of two classics creates a third, and this Classic Comics spin-off deserves an "A" for effort. What better way to present serious literature to children than to feature the kooky, inexplicably popular Heckle and Jeckle cartoon duo? Unfortunately, the issue was not successful. Readers found the concept of a crow drinking a potion and turning into an absolutely identical crow less than terrifying.

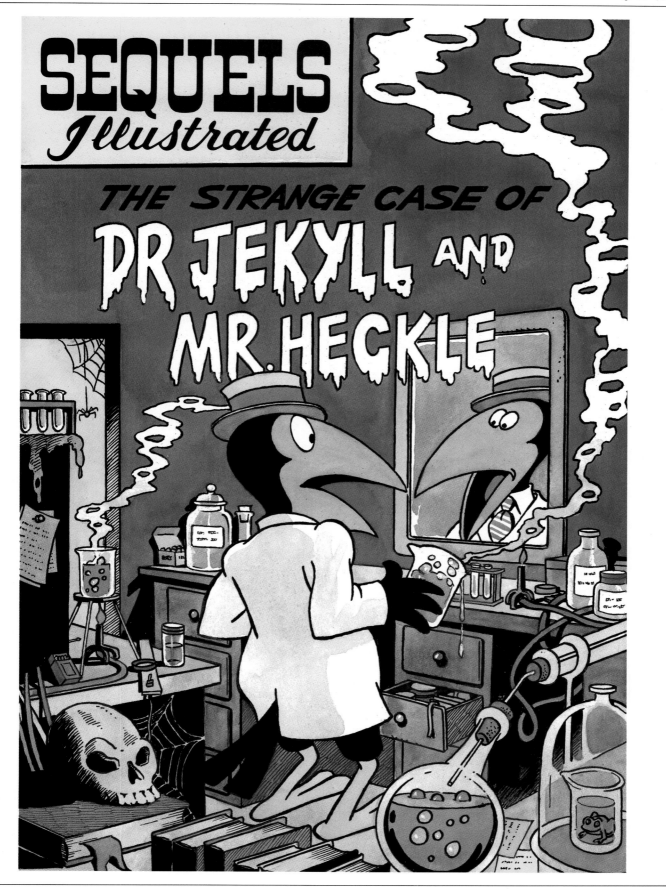

> *"Oh, do not ask 'What is it?'*
> *Let us go and make our visit."*
> —T.S. Eliot™

Welcome!

This Guidepamphlet should help you make the most of your visit to East St. Louis, Illinois (just across the river from T.S. Eliot's™ native city), and to our unique theme park, inspired by, and dedicated to, the memory and beloved poetry of the "Old Possum" himself, T.S. Eliot.™

Make a "pilgrimage" to our **Traditional Old World Cathedral!** Thrill to "Mr. Eliot's Sunday Morning Service," which includes the mystifying "Fire Sermon" as well as the shocking "Martyrdom of Beckett!"

Lose yourself in the mysterious **Chapel Perilous,** where "Romance is a Ritual!"

Do You Dare enter **Mr. Kurtz's House of Horrors?** On display: The Skull Beneath the Skin! The Murderous Paws of Rachel née Rabinowitz! Fear in a Handful of Dust!

While in **Dead Land,** visit the **Prickly Pear,** the world's tallest rotating tea room. (We go round at 5 a.m. daily.)

Beautiful hot gammon and oysters on the half shell are available at Lil and Albert's **Sawdust Restaurant** in **Unreal City.**

Try the breadfruit and fresh eggs served at the nice little, white little **Missionary Stew Pot,** located directly under the **Bamboo Tree** on **Cannibal Isle.**

Higher Entertainment Nightly:

Mermaids (sea girls wreathed in seaweed red and brown) sing for *you* at the underwater **Chambers of the Sea** lounge!

Live in Concert: "That Shakespeherian Rag," performed simultaneously by Four Quartets.

And don't miss the fabulous "Falling Shadow Show," presented perpetually in **Dead Land.**

Dead Land Legend
(see map):
1. The Idea.
2. The Reality.
3. The Motion.
4. The Act.

Your Host,

J. Alfred
"The Eternal Footman"
Prufrock

The Satanic Reverses

One evening in 1989, a tall blond woman, clad in an open-necked man's shirt and sporting several days' growth of scraggly beard, appeared at our New York offices waving a typed copy of the sequel reproduced below. "This was intended to be Book II of a two-part novel, Book I of which was The Satanic Verses," *she confided in a surprisingly deep whisper. "But the publisher forgot to include it in the finished edition. It was a terrible — in fact, a near fatal — error. Only you can correct it." She dropped her manuscript on the front desk, and before our dumbfounded night receptionist could respond, she was gone.*

Baal said, "I'm finished, do what you want."

So he was sentenced to be beheaded, within the hour, and as the soldiers manhandled him out of the tent toward the killing ground, he shouted over his shoulder: "Whores and writers, Mahound. We are the people you can't forgive."

Mahound replied, "Writers and whores. I see no difference here."

—Salman Rushdie
The Satanic Verses

Here he comes, Mahound, the businessman turned Prophet, climbing Mount Cone to receive a revelation from the "Archangel" Gibreel: Mahound, whose Devil-connoting name, coined in treachery by the early Christians, the Prophet *himself* adopted to turn insults into strengths (something his chronicler was *very* careful to point out on page 93 of *The Satanic Verses*).

Gibreel awaits him in their dream (*Yes,* he reminds himself, in our *dream!* It was only a dream Mahound and I shared last time, as our chronicler practically turned *somersaults* to make it plaintosee, and it's only a dream *now*, and a half-mad character's looney-tune dream at *that!*). Gibreel's fear, the fear of the self his dream creates (not to mention his chronicler's fear for his own safety), makes him struggle against Mahound's arrival. But Mahound has reached the summit now, no quesch, and it's time for Gibreel to make the speech of his life.

"Mahound," begins Gibreel, "remember that dream I you we had? The one with those verses in it that implied it would be O.K. with God if you permitted the elevation of three stone-idol goddesses to the status of archangels? Well, it was all a *terrible misunderstanding*, all right?—just a little joke that got an eensy bit out of control . . ."

"Relax, Gibreel," Mahound smiles. "I later renounced those verses as the work of *Shaitan*, remember? In fact, to make absolutely sure no one would miss the point, our chronicler based the title of his *entire novel* on this incident!"

"But it goes further than that, O.K.?" pants Gibreel. "There were *no Satanic verses* for you to renounce, do you understand? In fact, there was no *you* to renounce them: you—and *I* for that matter, at least in my god-damned-angel-of-god-persona—are just the gone-baboon ravings of a fictional Indian idiot-actor who got blasted out of a jumbo jet at Everest height and somehow survived the fall!"

"Hmmm," says Mahound, taken

NOTE: The alert reader may question why *The Satanic Reverses*, a traditional prose sequel, is hidden away here among the milestones of merchandising in our "Spin-offs" section, rather than occupying a more appropriate spot earlier in the book. We hasten to point out that our "misplacement" of this material was entirely intentional; we felt that, wedged in between the map of a glitzy new theme park and a rock 'em-sock 'em adventure comic, this provocative work might be less likely to attract the attention of someone inclined to undervalue our safety.

somewhat aback at the prospect of his nonexistence. ''And what about those prostitutes who took the names of my wives? I suppose they, too, were figments of a demented dream?''

"Ohé, Salad baba. . . . what-ho, old Chumch. Hey, Spoono, Dharrraaammm! Wham, na? What an entrance, yaar. I swear: splat . . ."

The ''Archangel'' is rolling now. ''Indeed they were!'' he enthuses. ''Not only was the mere dream existence of those prostitutes spelled out by our chronicler *in no uncertain terms* on page 376 of *The Satanic Verses;* it also would be obvious to anyone who had read that far into the novel that the prostitutes were designed to embody the *profane antithesis* of the message of God, and that our chronicler meant their scandalous behavior to *instruct,* not to *offend!''*

''Ah,'' says the Prophet Messenger Businessman, ''but isn't the problem that almost no one *did* read that far into the novel? And if I may say so, the fault, dear Gibreel, is largely yours. Even *I*—a product of the very same bugs-in-the-brain dream as you—had scarcely gotten past your infernal chant of 'Ho ji! Ho ji! Tat-taa! Taka-thun!'—*on the very first page of the book!*—before I slid, heavy-lidded, into a deep and torpid stupor.''

The chronicler, tormented and sweat-glistened in a bed between whose silken sheets he never expected to sleep, dreams a paradox: How unfortunate, his dream-self muses, that so few of the hundreds of thousands who purchased my great wheel of a book—including the Prophet Messenger Businessman I myself created—have ploughed through enough of it to grasp its epic meaning. But, then again, how *fortunate* that Mahound never read far enough to discover that, on page 546, Gibreel put the barrel of a gun into his own mouth and pulled the trigger, thereby rendering it impossible for him to appear on Mount Cone and recite the disclaimer credited to him in this new work.

And now suddenly the chronicler comes wide awake, eyes popping open in revelation. ''Mother-fucking dreams cause all the troubles of the human race,'' he hisses, ''especially those of glittering novelists such as myself. If I were God— and let there be no misunderstanding, I'd *never* make such a claim!—I'd cut the imagination right out of people and then maybe poor bastards like me could get a good night's rest.''

He yawns and stretches and begs *what? whom?* for untroubled, dreamless sleep. His fingers move absently along the surface of the table beside his bed and what should materialize in his hand but a copy of *The Satanic Verses,* and, yessir, it's turned to page one.

''Ohé, Salad baba, it's you, too good. What-ho, old Chumch,'' reads the chronicler. ''Hey, Spoono, *Dharrraaammm!* Wham, na? What an entrance, yaar. I swear: splat . . .'' And, even as he reaches the end of the page, hey presto he's overcome by warm, soporific heaviness, and, like the Messenger before him, he escapes, slowslow at first, then fasterfaster, into blessed unconsciousness. ⏻

Godot Action Comics

This monthly publication was part of an American Sequel Society campaign to convince today's sensation-seeking con- **sumers that even the most cerebral *chefs d'oeuvre* offer more than their fair share of ''thrills and excitement.''**

If the Apostle Paul didn't invent the evangelical epistle, he certainly popularized it. What is less widely known is that St. Paul also wrote the first chain letter—this spin-off of his popular sequel, The Second Epistle to the Corinthians.

The Chain Letter of Paul the Apostle to the Corinthians

WITH CHARITY ALL THINGS ARE POSSIBLE

This epistle comes to you from Philippi. Grace be to you and peace. Spiritual gifts will be delivered unto you within four days of receiving this letter—providing you in turn send it on.

2 This is no joke. Send copies to whomsoever among the gentiles you would comfort in all their tribulation. Do not send material things. Charity vaunteth not itself, is not puffed up.

3 While visiting the Household of Stephanas, a Macedonian proconsul received the epistle and was greeted by his brethren with a holy kiss. But he broke the chain, and now he is become as sounding brass or a tinkling cymbal.

4 Gaius bestowed all his goods to feed the poor, and gave his body to be burned, but it profited him nothing. He failed to circulate the letter. However, before his death, he received the unleavened bread of sincerity and truth.

5 Do note the following: Crispus had the gift of prophecy, and understood all mysteries, and all knowledge, and had all faith, so that he could remove mountains. But he forgot that the epistle had to leave his hands within 96 hours, and now he is nothing.

6 In A.D. 37, the epistle was received by a young Galatian woman who put it aside to copy and send out later. She was plagued by various problems: thrice she was beaten with rods, once she was stoned, and thrice suffered shipwreck. On the last of these occasions, she spent a night and a day in the deep. Finally, she copied the letter. A trumpet sounded, and she was raised incorruptible.

7 Remember: Believeth all things, hopeth all things. The chain never faileth.

St. Paul

Shortly after writing his Chain Letter to the Corinthians, Paul realized that, with a few minor improvements, the chain epistle could be a powerful fund-raising instrument for the Church. In his Memorandum to the Egyptians, the "Apostle of the Pagans" also reveals an intimate working knowledge of the swindle which, as a consequence of its being documented for the first time in this missive, has become known as the "Pyramid Scheme."

The Word-a-Day in the Life of Ivan Denisovich Calendar

During the period when Alexander Solzhenitsyn was still living in the Soviet Union and his manuscripts were being smuggled abroad for publication, several unauthorized spin-off products based on his gloomy but magisterial writings were released in the West, including The Gulag Archipelago Game, *The Siberian Strict Labor Regime Prison Camp Diet,* and this calendar.

delator

\di-'lā-tor\ *n:* one who denounces or accuses another; an informer

If the prisoners discovered that someone in their barracks was a *delator,* he would be found dead one morning with his throat slit.

Monday   January 15

ravenous

\'rav-ə-nəs\ *adj:* extremely and intensely hungry; famished; voracious

Since the inmates of the camp were fed only a hunk of bread, a bit of sugar, and three bowls of mush each day, they were always *ravenous.*

Tuesday   January 16

maleficent

\mə-'lef-ə-sənt\ *adj:* doing evil or causing harm; harmfully malicious

Most of the guards were just ordinary soldiers doing a job, but Lieutenant Volkovoy, the disciplinary officer, was genuinely *maleficent.*

Wednesday   January 17

fustigate

\'fus-ti-gāt\ *v t:* to cudgel; beat; club; bludgeon; punish severely

The mess-hall orderly they called Clubfoot had a big birch stick with which he would *fustigate* anyone who tried to go inside before he was given permission.

Thursday   January 18

contusion

\kən-'tōō-zhən\ *n:* an injury in which the subsurface tissue is damaged; a bruise

Fetyukov got beaten up for trying to scrounge somebody's food bowl, and he had a large *contusion* on the side of his face where he'd been hit.

Friday   January 19

hypothermia

\hi-pō-'thûr-mē-ə\ *n:* a physical condition characterized by subnormal body temperature

Ivan and Kilgas the Latvian stole a roll of roofing felt and nailed it over the empty window frames to keep the wind off the work gang so they wouldn't all get *hypothermia.*

Saturday   January 20

Adult Sequels

Ever mindful of our responsibility to bring great (and in a growing number of cases neglected) classics to a broad-based audience, the A-Double-S has recently created a series of home video sequels to great masterpieces especially tailored for dissemination in "adult" outlets. Following is a list of our initial offerings:

Across the River and Into Thérèse
And Quiet Flows the Dong
Appointment in Tamara
Arse Poetica
As I Lay Diane
The Ass Menagerie
As You Lick It
Beth Comes for the Archbishop
The Bugger's Opera
Captain Fellatio Hornblower
A Christmas in Carol
Cock Without Hands
David Cop a Feel
The Devil and Daniel Webster in Miss Jones
Eat Me in St. Louis
The Enema of the People
Five Little Peckers and How They Grew
Four Saints in Three Unnatural Acts
The Four Whoresmen of the Apocalypse
French the Lieutenant's Woman!
A Handful of Bust
Hedda Gobbler
Her Groin Was My Valley
He Stoops to Honk Her
The Innocents and a Broad
Inside Daisy Miller
Ivan's Ho'
Jude the Odd Screwer
Lady Windemere's Fanny
Lay Misérables
Lord Jism
The Lust of the Mohicans
Madame Ovary

Mansfield Pork
The Man Who Came on Dinner
A Member at the Wedding
Memoirs of a Fox-Humping Man
Moaning Becomes Electra
Moby-Dyke
The Naked in the Dead
Of Human Bondage and Discipline
Oh, Ye Jugs and Juleps
One Day in the Wife of Ivan Denisovich
The Penile Colony
Penis and Adonis
Pippa Pisses
The Pit and the Pudendum
Portrait of the Artist as a Hung Man
Pubic Enemy
The Rise of Silas' Lap
Rub in Some Crisco
The Satanic Nurses
The Shape of Things That Come
The Shlong of Roland
Strange Fruits
The Swish Family Robinson
A Tale of Two Clitties
Tales of a Wayside In and Out
Taras Vulva
Tess Does the D'Urbervilles
The Three Muffketeers
The Très Riches Whores of the Duc de Berry
Twat Makes Sammy Run
Uncle Ream Us
The Wife of Bath's Tail
Wrassle Ass

How They Faxed the Good News from Ghent to Aix

Recently, the American Sequel Society got the kind of call every cultural institution dreams of: a request from a Japanese advertising agency that we adapt Robert Browning's "How They Brought the Good News from Ghent to Aix" so that —without losing its linguistic beauty or artistic value—it would express the remarkable efficiency with which Toshiba facsimile machines handle major communications challenges. The resulting "sponsored sequel" appears here in book form for the first time.

I
I sprang 'cross my cubby, flipped on the machine
And, fixing my gaze on the LCD screen,
I inserted each page in the document tray;
When I'd finished SEND/READY lit up the display.

II
Then I lifted the handset, and listened awhile
Till a firm, steady buzz told me "Yes, you can dial";
When I'd punched in each digit, oh, how I was greeted:
The panel display spelled out DIALING COMPLETED!

III
A high, warbling shriek now emerged from the phone:
The distant facsimile's answering tone!
'Twas time to push START, so I depressed the key
And I prayed my transmission would be error-free.

IV
The machine leapt to action; a light flashed inside;
The rollers pulled each page in turn through the guide,
And my head filled with visions of some distant reader
Enjoying the news from my document feeder.

V
Then at last a beep told me, "Your memo got through!
No pages misfed, and no power supply blew;
No broken connection has ruined your call;
Neither your plug, nor theirs, has come loose from the wall."

VI
Yes, the news which alone could save Aix from her fate
Had arrived neatly stamped with my name and the date;
Now from their fax to mine a brief memo was sent
Saying "Thanks for transmitting such good news from Ghent!"

Existendo™ Video Games

Existentialist literature has never been a big hit with kids, and let's face it, would you slip Jean-Paul Sartre's Nausea into your beach bag? But the line of video games offered by the Existendo™ Company would put a wan smile on even Sartre's grouchy face. This screen from The Myth of Sisphus Game, and the accompanying excerpt from one of the firm's ads, say it all:

"Count on Existendo™ to bring you the very best in French Existentialist video games. Albert Camus' *Myth of Sisyphus* delivers endless hours of philosophically challenging, ego-battering entertainment. Ponder your pointlessness as Man scores big on the uphill push, then the Rock's downward roll sets him back to zip! Fruitless fun for the whole family.

●Also available : Sartre's enraging *No Exit*, Ionesco's action-free *Rhinoceros!*, and Beckett's depressing interactive video, *Krapp's Last Tape*. Buy them all! You'll be dead someday anyway!"

Literary Strips and Philosophical Funnies

BLOOMSBURY

This comic strip was written by Virginia Woolf and drawn by her artist-sister Vanessa Bell in 1920, a year in which the celebrated siblings, and indeed their entire "Bloomsbury" literary and artistic set, found themselves in need of some quick cash.

Intended as a lowbrow sequel to Virginia's opaquely confessional novels *The Voyage Out* and *Night and Day*, the strip ran in *Comic Cuts*, a widely circulated comic weekly

owned by Lord Northcliffe. Virginia's hopes that her work would find favor with "the common reader" were rudely dashed, and Northcliffe canceled his order after a single issue.

Woolf brooded about the failure of her "Bloomsbury" comic for the next two decades until, one day in 1941, she filled her pockets with stones, walked into the Atlantic, and drowned.

HOBBES AND CALVIN

As Richard Hofstader points out in *The American Political Tradition*, the U.S. Constitution is based upon the philosophy of Thomas Hobbes and the religion of John Calvin. It was only natural then that struggling artist Bill Watterson employed the two historic figures as "comic relief" characters in his proposed educational cartoon book, *A Beginner's Guide to Political Science*.

When the high-minded publishing firm which had originally commissioned his manuscript changed management and abruptly rejected it, the disillusioned Watterson lowered his sights somewhat and totally revamped his original work into a mass-market comic strip. Wealth and fame followed, and even Watterson himself soon forgot that the popular "Calvin and Hobbes" strip is, in fact, a sequel.

Like Chicago, Toronto suffers the denigrating nickname of "Second City." In a recent fit of boosterism, the governors of the Canadian metropolis paid a handsome stipend to a prominent local bard for the composition of the following "Official Poem of the Greater Metro Area."

Toronto

Hog carcass Grader for the World,
Deal Maker, Broker of Stocks,
Setter of Trends and the Nation's Preeminent Center,
Clean, modest, up-to-date,
City of the Sensible Apparel:
I hear you're pretty spicy, and I guess
maybe I believe it, eh, because I've
seen some of the R-rated films
available after midnight right in my
hotel room for a slight extra charge.
And I hear you're a bit full of yourself,
and I've got to admit, true enough,
I've seen those pseudos on the CBC
going on about some so-called art in
the Royal Ontario that any four-year-
old could draw better than.
And I also hear you aren't good value,
and to me, you'd better believe it,
even in the Malls everything is very
dear, from gas to groceries, and rents
are going through the roof all over the
whole Metro area.
And then I turn around and give it right
back to them. I say, So, big deal, get
over it, eh?
I suppose you can show me another city
with a free-standing pre-stressed
concrete structure you can take an
elevator to a world-class rotating
restaurant on the top of that's taller
than the CN Tower?
Telecasting first-rate programs, world-
class news and variety-
entertainment, comedy, talk shows,

distinctive Canadian Culture, here's
a stand-up defenseman facing a two-
on-one,
Heads-up like a real Maple Leaf, a team
player, a professional, not afraid to
play physical but seldom penalized
for unsportsmanlike conduct,
Helmet wearing,
Back checking,
Cutting down the angles,
Taking no chances,
Anticipating, reacting, not
committing himself,
Ready if he has to to go down and block
a shot at the last minute if he has to,
even if it hits him right in the mouth,
Increasingly aware of his wily
challengers for national power, but
still preeminent, and wearing that
smile,
Smiling the way a Toronto Dominion
Bank assistant loan officer smiles
who has never given anybody a loan,
Self-assured and smiling because under
his feet is the ground, and under his
arse is the center of Canada.
Smiling!
Smiling the clean, modern,
sophisticated smile of preeminence;
sensibly dressed, smirking, quite
content to be Hog carcass Grader,
Deal Maker, Broker of Stocks, Setter
of Trends and Center of Canadian
business, finance, culture, fashion,
and communications.

Among the author's many sources of inspiration we may mention not only Carl Sandburg's celebrated "Chicago," but also *Canada 1940, The Official Handbook, New York World's Fair Edition*, which notes (page 78), "Of considerable interest in Canadian hog marketing is the trend toward carcass grading," as well as a passage from Andrew H. Malcolm's *The Canadians* (Times Books, 1986): "Increasingly aware of its wily challengers for national power sits Toronto… the preeminent center of Canadian business, finance, culture, fashion, and communications."

With this thrilling "mix'n'match" activity, you can create more than 1,000,000—that's right, 1,000,000!—blockbuster follow-ups of your very own, covering the whole spectrum of literature and film.

Make Your Own Sequel™

NEW BEGINNINGS, NEXT CHAPTERS, AND CONTINUING NIGHTMARES

To give you a sense of how we at the American Sequel Society come up with all our fabulous ideas for follow-ups, we've designed a patented game that will enable you—our readers—to create your very own sequels! Simply choose a "beginning" from Column A, a "middle" from Column B, and an "end" from Column C, combine the phrases you've selected, and—presto! you've got your first "can't miss" book or movie. (For a shorter title, pick one from Column A and one from Column B; or one from Column B and one from Column C.) That's all there is to it!

BEGINNINGS

Abbott and Costello Meet
After
Alfred Hitchcock Presents:
Alias
Another Side of
Back to
The Bad News Bears in
The Bawdy Adventures of
Beneath the Planet of
The Best of
Beyond
Beyond the Valley of
Black
Blame It On
The Bowery Boys Meet
The Bride of
Carry On,
Castle of
Cheech and Chong's
Children of
Christmas with
Clan of
Codename:
Come Back,
The Confessions of
The Curse of
A Date with
The Daughter of
Dawn of
Deeper Inside
Disco
Escape from
The Essential
Frankenstein Meets
The Further Adventures of
The Fury of
The Genius of
Get
The Ghost of
Godzilla vs.
The Hardy Boys Discover
The Horror of
I Married

MIDDLES

Abie's Irish Rose
Antigone
Antony and Cleopatra
Attila the Hun
Babar
Adam Bede
Brunhilde
Caligula
the Cat in the Hat
Camille
Charlie's Aunt
Lady Chatterly
El Cid
Humphrey Clinker
a Connecticut Yankee
Death
the Dirty Dozen
a Dog of Flanders
Lorna Doone
Nancy Drew
the Duchess of Malfi
Quentin Durward
Jane Eyre
the Faerie Queen
Faust
the Finzi-Continis
Moll Flanders
Frodo
Ethan Frome
Hedda Gabler
Garfield
Garp
the Glass Family
Mr. Goodbar
the Great Gatsby
Hajji Baba of Ispahan
Hannah and Her Sisters
Herbie the Love Bug
Hiawatha
Hitler
Hogan's Goat
the House of Atreus
Jason

ENDS

: The Adventure Continues
: American Style
in the Army
: The Art of the Deal
: Assignment Miami Beach
and the Bachelor
, the Bad and the Ugly
and the Bandit
, the Barbarian
's Big Score
at Carnegie Hall
and Carol and Ted and Alice
and the Casino of Gold
's Children
and the Co-eds
Conquers the Universe
's Daughter
: The Day After
, The Destroyer
, Detective
of Dune
and the Dweebs
: The Early Days
's Excellent Adventure
: The Final Chapter
: The Final Frontier
's Ghost
in Girl Trouble
and the Gladiators
, the God
Goes Hawaiian
Goes Nutzoid
's Greatest Case
and the Green Goddess
: Happy at Last!
Has Risen from the Grave!
, the Heretic
at Home
on Ice
: An Introduction
: Italian Style
Joins the WACS
, Jr.

BEGINNINGS

Inside
Isaac Asimov Presents:
Island of
I Was a Teenage
Jesse James Meets
The Joy of
Kill
Kiss of
Kramer vs.
The Last Days of
Leave It to
The Legend of
Love Finds
Ma and Pa Kettle Meet
The Making of
The Mark of
Meet
Mondo
My Name Is Still
My Stepmother Is
The Mystery of
National Lampoon's
The New Adventures of
The Possession of
The Private Life of
Quotations from Chairman
Rainbow Brite and
The Return of
The Revenge of
The Rise and Fall of
The Road to
The Search for
The Secret of
Seven Brides for
The Seventh Voyage of
The Sins of
The Son of
The Song of
A Stone for
The Strange Case of
The Sword of
Tarzan Finds
Terror of
They Call Me
They Still Call Me
The Trial of
The Triumph of
Tropic of
Two Mules for
Under
Viva!
Walt Disney's
Whatever Happened to
The Wit and Wisdom of
The Wrath of
Young
Zorro and

MIDDLES

Joan of Arc
Jude the Obscure
Anna Karenina
Lancelot
Lassie
Abe Lincoln
Studs Lonigan
Mack the Knife
Maggie: A Girl of the Streets
le Malade Imaginaire
Silas Marner
Mary, Queen of Scots
The Master of Ballantrae
The Mayor of Casterbridge
Daisy Miller
Marjorie Morningstar
the Mummy
the Nigger of the Narcissus
Ninotchka
the Noble Savage
Oedipus
the Partridge Family
Pericles, Prince of Tyre
Porgy and Bess
Portnoy
Hester Prynne
Quasimodo
Captain Queeg
Rebecca of Sunnybrook Farm
Riki-tiki-tavi
Robin Hood
Sabu, the Elephant Boy
Salome
the Scarlet Pimpernel
Bart Simpson
Sinbad
the Snopeses
Steppenwolf
Swann
Tom Swift
the Three Amigos
Trilby
Troilus and Cressida
Kilgore Trout
Nat Turner
the Two Mrs. Grenvilles
Uncle Tom
Uncle Vanya
the Undead
the Velveteen Rabbit
the Vicar of Wakefield
the Wandering Jew
the Whore of Babylon
the Yearling
Dr. Zhivago
Zorba the Greek
Zuckerman

ENDS

vs. Kramer
, Live at the Hollywood Bowl
's Little Dividend
Lives!
and the Lost City of Gold
: A Love Story
Mania!
on Mars
vs. Megalon
, Messiah
and the Mole Men
, Mon Amour
: The Musical
: The Never Ending Story
: A New Beginning
: The Next Day
: The Next Generation
: The Nightmare Continues
: One Million, B.C.
: One More Time
at the Opera
in Orbit
: The Original Nightmare
of Oz
on Panther Island
: Part 2
: The Rebirth
Redux
: The Reincarnation
: The Reunion
Revisited
on the Rocks
's Savage Fury
's School Days
at Sea
's Secret
and the Sins of Babylon
vs. the Smog Monster
's Song
Strikes Back
: The Sun Sessions
, Superstar
: Surviving at the Top
and the Temple of Doom
in the 25th Century
2
II
II: Your Sister Is a Werewolf
2000
—Unchained!
Under the Sea
on Vacation
and His Vampire Brides
and the Voice of Terror
, Who Will Be 25 in the Year 2000
's Widow
Without Tears

The *Make Your Own Sequel*™ game is lots of fun; and it can also be lucrative! You're absolutely free to sell any or all of the sequels you come up with, without any obligation to us (although we'd love to hear your success stories—drop us a line!).

Index of Credits

FRONT COVER
Illustration by Leslie Cabarga
Title lettering by Alex Jay

ADULT SEQUELS
Conceived by Sean Kelly and
Chris Kelly
Created by Sean Kelly, Chris Kelly,
Christopher Cerf, Henry
Beard, Sarah Durkee, and
Michael Frith

**ANSWERS TO THE LETTERS
OF GEORGE BERNARD SHAW**
Written by Christopher Cerf and
Henry Beard

ARISTOTLE'S AEROBICS
Conceived by Henry Beard and
Sean Kelly
Written by Christopher Cerf,
Henry Beard, and Sean Kelly
Photographed by John E. Barrett
Models: Lisa Lawton and
Phillip Germano
Title lettering designed by
Diane Bertolo
Title lettering executed by Alex
Jay, Robert Rakita and
David Kaestle
Costumes designed by
Deborah Lombardi
Stylist: Louisa Grassi

BACK WITH THE WIND
Introduction written by
Sarah Durkee
Title lettering design by David
Kaestle and Diane Bertolo

**THE BIG FAT
BALDING PRINCE**
Written by Sarah Durkee
Illustrated by Warren Sattler
Title lettering by Diane Bertolo

BLOOMSBURY
Conceived and written by
Sean Kelly
Comic strip art by Warren Sattler

**BRIDESHEAD REVISITED
REVISITED**
Written by Henry Beard

**A BRIEF HISTORY OF ART
AND ARCHITECTURE
SEQUELS**
Written by Henry Beard
Captions by Sarah Durkee and
Henry Beard
Art and photo research by
Louisa Grassi and
Laura McFarland-Taylor

**CASEY II: IT AIN'T OVER TILL
IT'S OVER**
Written by Christopher Cerf

**THE CHAIN LETTER OF PAUL
THE APOSTLE TO THE
CORINTHIANS**
Conceived by Henry Beard and
Christopher Cerf
Written by Christopher Cerf

THE COLOR SCARLETT
Written by Chris Kelly

DEAD BISON
Conceived by Henry Beard
Cave painting artifact by
David Kaestle

**THE DIVORCE OF THE
ARNOLFINIS**
Conceived by Henry Beard and
Christopher Cerf
Painting modifications by
Wayne McLoughlin

DIURETICS
Conceived by Sean Kelly and
Christopher Cerf
Copy written by Sean Kelly and
Christopher Cerf
Title Lettering by Ken Lopez

THE EATEN GYPSY
Conceived by Henry Beard
Painting modifications by
Robert Rakita

**THE EGYPTIAN FLIP BOOK
OF THE DEAD**
Conceived by Henry Beard,
Christopher Cerf and
Sean Kelly
Introduction written by
Sarah Durkee
Animated by Diane Bertolo, Dave
Wilson, and Donna Cisan

**THE EMPEROR OF FROZEN
YOGURT**
Conceived by Henry Beard
Written by Sarah Durkee

EXISTENDO™ VIDEO GAMES
Conceived by Christopher Cerf
and Henry Beard
Introduction and advertising
copy by Sarah Durkee
Video game graphic by
Natasha Lessnik

FINN FIN
Written by Sean Kelly

FIRST COMMUNION
Conceived by Sarah Durkee
Cover illustration by
James Bennett

FORCE 10 FROM CASABLANCA
Conceived by Sean Kelly, Henry
Beard and Christopher Cerf
Poster art by Jim Sharpe

GENESIS II
Conceived and written by
Norman Stiles
Art by Donna Diamond
Calligraphy by Ahza Moore

GODOT ACTION COMICS
Conceived and written by
Christopher Cerf
Art by Russ Heath
Lettering by Alex Jay, Ken Lopez,
and Russ Heath

**GO KINDLY AND GENTLY
INTO THAT GOOD NIGHT**
Written by Sarah Durkee

HOBBES AND CALVIN
Conceived and written by
Sean Kelly
Comic strip art by Warren Sattler

**HOW THEY FAXED THE GOOD
NEWS FROM GHENT TO AIX**
Conceived by Henry Beard
Written by Christopher Cerf

THE IDIOT SEQUELS
Written by Henry Beard
Photography by John E. Barrett
Prop fabrication by David Vogler
and Daniel O'Brien

I WAS A TEENAGE BEOWULF
Conceived by Sarah Durkee
Poster art by Jim Sharpe
Copy written by Henry Beard and
Christopher Cerf
Title lettering by David Vogler
and Ken Lopez

**JUDAISM AND THE ART OF
MOTORCYCLE MAINTENANCE**
Written by John Korkes and
Norman Stiles

**THE LIBRARY OF YIDDISH
SEQUELS**
Conceived by Sean Kelly and
Chris Kelly
Copy written by Christopher Cerf
Sequels created by Sean Kelly,
Christopher Cerf, Chris Kelly,
Henry Beard, Sarah Durkee,
and Norman Stiles
Photography by John E. Barrett
Stylist: Louisa Grassi

**THE LIGHTER SIDE OF
SYLVIA PLATH**
Written by Sarah Durkee

MAKE YOUR OWN SEQUEL™
Conceived by Sean Kelly
Created by Sean Kelly,
Christopher Cerf, Henry
Beard, and Sarah Durkee

**THE MAN WHO WOULD
BE QUEEN**
Conceived by Sean Kelly and
Danny Abelson
Written by Sean Kelly

**MOBY-DICK II: RAISE THE
PEQUOD!**
Story by Henry Beard and
Christopher Cerf
Written by Henry Beard
Cover illustration by
Wayne McLoughlin
Computer graphics/illustrations
by Diane Bertolo

**MOVIE SEQUELS/
THE ROCKY AWARDS**
Introduction written by
Christopher Cerf
"Rocky" silhouette by
Emma Crawford

**NUDE REASCENDING
A STAIRCASE**
Conceived by Henry Beard
Painting by Marcel Duchamp

**NUMBER ONE, WITH A
BULLET**
Introduction written by
Sean Kelly

THE ONE BULLET MANAGER
Written by Henry Beard
Cover graphics by Ken Pisani and
David Vogler

PET SEMINARY
Conceived by Sarah Durkee
Cover illustration by
James Bennett

**PRIDE AND EXTREME
PREJUDICE**
Conceived by Henry Beard
Cover art modification by
Wayne McLoughlin
Caption by Christopher Cerf

THE PRINCESS
Written by Henry Beard

PUJO
Conceived by Sarah Durkee
Cover illustration by Rudy Laslo

**THE RETURN OF THE GIFT
OF THE MAGI**
Conceived by Henry Beard and
Christopher Cerf
Written by Christopher Cerf

THE ROAD TAKEN
Written by Sean Kelly

**ROMEO AND JULIET, PART 1
(CONT.)**
Written by Henry Beard
Frontispiece graphics by
Diane Bertolo

THE SATANIC REVERSES
Written by Christopher Cerf
Cover graphics by Ken Pisani
Persian miniature by
Jack Woolhiser

THE SCARLETT FANNY
Written by Sarah Durkee

**SIR GAWAIN AND THE GREEN
KNIGHT AT THE OPERA**
Conceived by Sean Kelly and
Chris Kelly
Written by Sean Kelly
Engraving art by
Mikhail Ivenitsky

THE SLAP
Conceived by Henry Beard,
Christopher Cerf, and
Sarah Durkee
Photo retouching by
Robert Rakita

SLAVES OF ATLANTA
Written by Sarah Durkee

**SOLITUDE: THE NEXT
ONE HUNDRED YEARS**
Written by Henry Beard
Cover illustration by Peter Fiore

SOUTHERN BELLEFLEUR
Written by Chris Kelly
Title lettering by Ken Lopez

**SPIN-OFFS/
CULTURE: THE NEXT
GENERATION**
Introduction written by
Christopher Cerf

**THE STEPHEN KING
BOOK-OF-THE-WEEK CLUB**
Conceived by David Rosenthal
Captions by Christopher Cerf

**THE STRANGE CASE OF
DR. JEKYLL AND MR. HECKLE**
Conceived by Sean Kelly
Comic cover by Warren Sattler
Caption by Sarah Durkee

THAT'S RE-ENTERTAINMENT
Written by Henry Beard

**THUS JOKED ZARATHUSTRA
(ALSO SPASST ZARATHUSTRA)**
Written by Henry Beard

TORONTO
Conceived by Henry Beard and
Sean Kelly
Written by Sean Kelly

TREES II-XLVI
Written by Sean Kelly,
Christopher Cerf, and
Henry Beard

**T.S. ELIOT'S™ WASTELAND
THEME PARK**
Conceived by Henry Beard
Created by Sean Kelly,
Christopher Cerf, Henry
Beard, and Sarah Durkee
Map and illustrations by
Gary Hallgren

**TWO CITIES II: THE
TALE CONTINUES**
Written by Henry Beard

2000: A SPACE ILIAD
Conceived by Sean Kelly
Poster art by Wayne McLoughlin
Caption by Henry Beard

VEGETABLE FARM
Conceived Sarah Durkee
Cover graphics Ken Pisani
Caption by Sarah Durkee

**THE VISITOR ORIENTATION
CENTER AT THE
GREAT PYRAMID AT GIZA**
Conceived by Henry Beard,
Christopher Cerf, and
Sarah Durkee
Photo retouching by
Robert Rakita

THE WAY THINGS BREAK
Conceived and written by
Sarah Durkee
Illustrated by William Ruggieri

**WHAT I SCRIBE—
HERE IN AMHERST**
Written by Sean Kelly

**THE WORD-A-DAY IN THE
LIFE OF IVAN DENISOVICH
CALENDAR**
Conceived by Henry Beard and
Christopher Cerf
Written by Henry Beard
Graphics by Diane Bertolo

**THE WORLD TRADE CENTER
AT PISA**
Conceived by Henry Beard,
Christopher Cerf, and
Sarah Durkee
Photo retouching by
Robert Rakita